ACTING UP!

an Innovative Approach to

Creative Drama

for Older Adults

by

**MARCIE TELANDER
FLORA QUINLAN
KAROL VERSON**

Coach House Press, Inc.
Chicago

ACTING UP!

An Innovative Approach to Creative Drama for Older Adults

by

Marcie Telander
Flora Quinlan
Karol Verson

Library of Congress Cataloging in Publication Data

Telander, Marcie 1946-
Quinlan, Flora 1950-
Verson, Karol 1939-
  ACTING UP!

Catalog Card No.: 81-71391
ISBN: 0-88020-108-8

Manufactured in the United States of America

Designed by Sterling Graphics
Cover photo by Mark Schwiesow

THE COACH HOUSE PRESS, INCORPORATED, Publishers
53 West Jackson Blvd., Chicago, Illinois 60604
Telepho...

TABLE OF CONTENTS

In loving memory of Shirley Helfand,
and
To those vital people who continue to make
ACTING UP! a joyous, transforming
part of growing older

ACTING UP! IN THE BEGINNING

Stand with me at mid-day, in the open, where the sun casts no shadow, and let us together consider all things concerning our art—that which lies ahead of us—the great promise of it, and that which lies close about us and claims our immediate attention. I would have you know that tingling mood which comes to all who share the best that they have found.

Izaak Walton, *The Compleat Angler*

The ACTING UP! process was created out of a certain innocence, the brand of innocence that allowed its leaders the opportunity to innovate without many of the preconceived notions or professional debates that those experienced in the science of gerontology or traditional theater may have encountered.

This is not to say that there weren't failures along the way, momentary doubts, occasional bad timing and hopes which went unfulfilled. But through all of our growth and discovery we believed that the art of theatre, a populist theatre to which we were all dedicated, would bring forth a process accessible to many, and perhaps even products beyond those we had first imagined.

When I speak of innocence, I speak of my own initial experiences while founding the ACTING UP! troupe which has continued to create and perform for the last six years through the excellent leadership of subsequent directors, Flora Quinlan and Karol Verson.

I had taught various adult education courses for "Senior Citizens" through community colleges in the Chicago area. But these were standard fare designed years ago as sedentary traditional courses— discussion of literature, film and drama. I found myself being energized by many of the older people whom I met through my teaching, and their general comment was always to ask for something new, and more and more of it. Being interested in improvisational techniques as a writer and actor I began to try some of these activities in my traditional classroom situations—and the results were not to be ignored. Whether it was storytelling, or more active theatre games, the people in my classes were willing and interested. They were humorous, eccentric, opinionated, rich with experience, and once opened to this type of theatre, challenged me to tap their amazing stores of raw materials and personal resources.

I had spent several years collecting folklore and oral literature whenever I had an opportunity, in nursing homes, poetry classes, schools, retirement hotels and hot meals programs. The writer in me was fascinated. I was thrilled with the art form that I recognized here, the vanishing art of storytelling, and the teller's ability to bring personal experiences vividly to life. Without props, a written script or stage, small enthralling dramas were being spun all around me.

I would sit with my tape recorder in the recreation areas, card rooms and libraries of retirement hotels and listen to the mesmerizing stories of seventy, eighty, and ninety year-old immigrants, professionals, family black sheep, laborers, con men, great-grandmothers and streetwise philosophers. When a story was truly rich, the teller would forget himself and stand up, gesturing, moving about, speaking in dialects from the old country, the southside of Chicago, Georgia or the Arkansas hills and the drab recreation room would become a stage. Sometimes in these exciting tellings, one of the other residents who had heard the story before, or who had a concurrent experience to share would join in the telling, acting out her part as she went along. Dialogue would grow and build and the scene would come to life. Often there were tears of laughter, or heads nodding solemnly at a sad tale that many had experienced, and often there would be applause. The storyteller would pause, realizing that he or she had held the audience spellbound, and something magical would occur. These people who lived together and believed that they knew all there was to know about each other had discovered something grand. They had discovered the theatre which arises from communicating our shared experiences, and they had discovered the natural actors in themselves.

Again, in my innocence, I believed that all that was necessary at this point was to launch wholesale into improvisational drama activities. I soon discovered that a great deal of careful groundwork was necessary before personal story-tellings could translate gracefully into a more active form of theatre.

The first unofficial group of elders with whom I worked showed me that it would take thoughtful planning and encouragement, ongoing individual and group support and all the energy I could muster to help them recognize how important what they had experienced, and what they had to say about growing older in today's world were to their peers and to younger people like myself.

This was my first experience in leading groups made up solely of people over the age of sixty-five. I had always loved hearing the stories that my grandparents told, and in the theatre and in teaching I had worked with mature actors and adults returning to school. But I had a great deal to learn about the needs and concerns of that important group from which I, as so many people, had been separated for most of my life.

Often I was afraid. I knew so much less about the world than they did. The false and destructive myths of ageism affect us all, regardless of our ages, and I was learning to face my personal fears of growing old. But through the generosity and patience of the elders I was learning the exhilaration that occurs when age limits and distinctions drop away and universal experiences emerge to unite us.

Fortunately, I was attempting something for which I found few guidelines and few precursors. Without the inhibitions imposed by traditional disciplines, we were free to experiment, make mistakes, try again, and reach for innovative answers to our problems. I always received encouragement in the development of this process from the older individuals who guided me along the way.

From the beginning there were many professionals in the field of education, gerontology, psychology and drama who had serious doubts that a project of this nature could be successful. Perhaps it is difficult to imagine that it took almost four years of searching for an innovative and humanistic educational institution, and a concerned Office on Aging before I was able to contact those individuals who were truly able to visualize and believe in the project. But in the early seventies in the Chicago area, and in many other parts of the country, the idea of vital progressive arts programs for senior adults were considered frivolous or less important than education for more traditional students. Groups such as Jacqueline Sunderland's National Center on Arts and the Aging, Gay Luce's SAGE project, Patrick Henry's Free Street Theater, David Shepherd's Improvisation Olympics and the University of Baltimore's Autumn Players were unique in their advocacy of quality programs for elders and younger generations working together.

Again I was fortunate. Patricia R. Handzel, Director of the Community Outreach Program of Oakton Community College, now in

Des Plaines, Illinois, and sponsor of our program, spared nothing to see that this project would be given a chance to live and continue to grow. She taught me that collaboration between community organizations is an important focus for such projects. Peg Gilmour, Director of the Skokie Office on Aging and co-sponsor of our first workshops, proved that truly creative and concerned Senior Center administrators will make resources, support and endless encouragement available to programs which offer quality experiences for elders. Local and state arts councils as well as Oakton Community College assisted us with start-up funding, publicity and space for some of our rehearsals. Dedicated people such as Vivian Mitchell of Oakton Community College, ACTING UP! Business Manager for five years, have given unsparingly of their time and energy.

In the spirit of collaboration the ACTING UP! program was begun. And it has continued to draw its greatest strength and support from the group's ability to reach out to many different individuals and institutions.

In developing your own program for older adults you will find that similar support is always available. By bringing together various community organizations you can benefit a broader range of individuals in your community while strengthening the base upon which you plan to build your program.

Our program was offered to those interested and over the age of sixty in the suburban Skokie area and surrounding communities. No auditions were held, no acting experience was required, and throughout all of our workshop sessions no one was turned away. Instead, our policy was to help the group remain flexible so that it could grow and change to accommodate new members.

Some of the members of our group had already become briefly acquainted with one another through activities at the Office on Aging where we were meeting. Others had wandered into the group from meetings in other parts of the Senior Center. And a few members were new to the Skokie area and had come to meet others in their community.

The atmosphere at the opening of the first meeting was tense and formal. Almost everyone addressed his or her neighbor as "Mr. This" or "Mrs. That." I allowed ten minutes for social formalities as the group felt its way into the meeting. Rather than asking each individual to introduce himself or herself, we split up into *Introduction Duos* to give people a chance to begin intensive listening activities, which would be a cornerstone for all of our work to follow.

Our first two months of meetings were at the Skokie Office on Aging in a rather small crowded, multi-purpose room. We met for two hours, once each week. Our meeting was held after a group called "Busy Hands" had its workshop. Long tables filled the room where women sat, chatting and knitting, crocheting, making afghans or fancy clothes for their grandchildren's dolls. This was not necessarily a place that lent itself to an easy transformation into a stage. But the word "transformation" began to have a special meaning for us, even beyond its important use in theatre. This is a word which I believe can help you in understanding the simplicity and power of creative problem-solving upon which you will be building the ACTING UP! process.

Some of the people in the workshop had never seen a play. Only one had had some acting experience—in a high school play. Others came to the group not understanding that a commitment of time and energy beyond a Senior Center social gathering would be requested. And everyone had rigid inhibitions and fears about the idea of "performing" and "acting." Our first meetings were given over to discussions in which we talked about retirement, family, society and politics and discussed at length the dangers of stereotyping older people and the cultural short-hand which is often applied to people over sixty-five.

We listed many of the myths of aging that affected us. It was then that we agreed that "bursting the myths of ageism"—ageism as it affects younger people as well as the older generation—would be the main focus of our dramatic work.

These sessions spent talking were important. They were necessary to build a sense of "trust" because the members of the group were learning to feel confident in expressing their thoughts and feelings verbally to people they had never met before. From the very first session we began filming and recording the group for the documentary film of ACTING UP!, and the taped transcripts of the group's discussions provided me and the members with many of the raw materials we would later use in our improvisations and vignettes.

As I look back at the documentary film, *ACTING UP!*, which I made with filmmaker Mark Schwiesow documenting the two and one-half years I directed the group, I am able to see how much the seven members who are still with the performance group have changed from our very first meetings. I am also aware of all the learning I had yet to gather from the members of the group in those early stages.

What we discovered in creating with many different groups of people in ACTING UP! workshops and seminars is that regardless of economic or cultural background, the ACTING UP! process does work. Out of all that we have learned and experienced with the elders' and intergenerational programs that we have led, the most important realization is that there is an area of commonality, a human connective tissue between life and drama that makes our storytellings, story-theatre performances and improvisations speak a universal language—ageless, timeless, without nationality or geographic boundaries.

The purpose of the ACTING UP! process is to assist in empowering older individuals with the confidence and abilities which lead to creative self-expression. And so, after almost ten years in development—learning and teaching, experimenting, failing, succeeding and refining techniques gathered from many sources—these are the most effective steps we have discovered in bringing the ACTING UP! process to others.

Marcie Telander
Founding Director
Chicago, Illinois 1982

BURSTING THE MYTHS OF AGEISM

> In the environment of their new leisure the aging have
> suffered intensely from society's indifference toward
> their untapped creative powers.
>
> Jacqueline Sunderland
National Center on Arts and
the Aging
National Council on the Aging

In the last decade many euphemistic phrases have been coined to identify those of us over the age of sixty: Long-Livers, Mature Adults, Older Americans, Senior Citizens. This urge to give a specially defined position to twelve per cent of the population is significant. In our culture, we are ambivalent toward those who have lived in this world the longest. We feel the need to isolate our elders, not only actually, by placing them outside of the mainstream of society's activities, but symbolically, by creating special names and phrases which hold older people apart from the rest.

We live, as Alfred Stieglitz once said, "in a country that is in love with standardization." And so we tend to consciously or unconsciously support the unfounded designation attached to our oldest generations, "no longer in the work force, no longer youthful in appearance, no longer closely involved with the rearing of a family—therefore, no longer a useful part of the *standard society.*"

And yet, strong traces of historical and cultural pride remain in our response to our elders. We come from roots, no matter how disparate, which remind us of the respect and reverence former generations gave to those members of the community, tribe or family who had lived and experienced the most through the distinction of age.

A coal miner's wife in a small town in Colorado who has lived through more than eighty harsh winters of chopping wood, shovelling snow and teaching in an isolated country school made this comment:

> ...so, they've decided to call us Senior Citizens now, eh? That word Senior always meant a lot to me: A Senior in high school, Senior army officer, a Senior official. It was something to work for and be proud of. Why is it now that I'm finally a *Senior*—other folks don't seem to see it as the achievement I do?

We isolate people over the age of sixty in many ways. By assuming that physical debilitation and mental incapacitation automatically accompany aging, we deny older citizens the opportunity to work if they so choose, thus excluding them from the marketplace and political structure which they helped to build. By creating living situations which separate our elders from the rest of society we discourage personal freedom, independence, the confidence to take risks and creativity in our fellow citizens, as well as our elders.

Through these actions we have efficiently separated ourselves from at least two generations who have experienced some of the most important changes ever to take place in the history of civilization. We have segregated the energetic forward-looking people who helped to make many of those changes become reality. Sadly, we have collaborated in denying ourselves a wealth of knowledge and a spirit of individualism that is sorely needed in today's world. In many ways we are denying the importance of our own past, and thus endangering our future.

Throughout the following activities the "myths of ageism" will be referred to as material ripe for discussion and transformation into positive dramatic statements. Of course this list is not complete, but these are among the falsehoods, stereotypes and prejudices which have affected elders, their attitudes about themselves and society's attitudes and treatment of them in both subtle and obvious ways. We cannot ignore them if we are to declare an end to isolation and misunderstanding. You will want to return often to these statements as you continue to add from your group's own personal observations and experience. This list was drawn from our discussions and such sources as Hugh Downs' book, *Thirty Dirty Lies about Old!** and the National Council on the Aging free pamphlet, *Facts and Myths about Aging.*** We strongly suggest that you make these materials freely available to the members of your group.

Among ACTING UP! members the following myths engendered lively discussions, writing and dramatic improvisations based upon the origins, problems and possible solutions to ageism:

Old people are all alike; are poor; live all alone; can't function in society; are sick; are depressed; can't cut the mustard; are a drag on everybody else.

After sixty-five, everyone goes steadily downhill.

Old age is a time of relative peace and serenity when people can relax and enjoy the fruits of their labors after the storms of active life are over.

Older people can no longer produce on a job or be active socially or creatively.

The notion of sexuality beyond the seventies is shameful and perverse. Old people do not have sexual desires, could not make love if they wanted to, are too fragile, are physically unnattractive, and are therefore sexually undesirable.

30 Dirty Lies (Niles, IL: Argus Communication, 1979)
**NCOA, 600 Maryland Ave., S.W., Washington, D.C. 20024

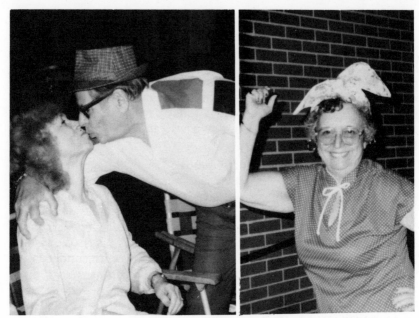

Most seniors are senile, rigid in thought and old-fashioned in morality and skills.

Old people conceal their age from themselves as well as others. Older people want to be young again.

The aging are past their prime.

Old age means you will go deaf, lose your sight, lose your balance, and waste away.

Older people cannot understand or relate to what younger people are thinking or doing.

Old people are useless; they can no longer be effective workers.

Old people do not like a lot of excitement. They like to be peaceful and quiet. They cannot handle any kind of pressure.

Old people are inflexible and refuse to try anything new.

Old people are too demanding and want everything done their way.

An old person is an *old* person (perjorative connotation).

Old people can't keep track of family relationships.

You can't teach an old dog new tricks.

Older people stand little chance in a country that accents youth.

Arthritis is a disease of old people.

Intelligence declines with age.

People beyond seventy are too old to have a pilot's license (or a driver's, a beautician's, you-name-it license).

Old people are eccentric.

Time goes faster when you're old.

Retirement will kill you.

Old people need less (of everything).

Face it: if you are old, you're bound to be ripped off.

It's bad to dwell on the past.

People are what they are, so it's useless to try to change attitudes toward the elderly.

Now it is your challenge as a creative group to reestablish the positive aspects of growing older. In ACTING UP! we capitalize on our strengths—wisdom, experience, understanding, intelligence, love and physical vitality. Our goal is to rediscover ourselves and move to reclaim our rightful, powerful place in the world.

> As an elder you realize you are no longer turned inward as if in a cocoon reacting to everything around you. Maturity is a feeling of consideration for other people around you no matter what their station in life.
>
> Tom Burns

CONSIDERING
THE ART OF LEADERSHIP

The Hopi never talks about "art." It is a way of life
with him. He believes that each person, before he is
born is conscious of art and music and dance. If he is
aware of the balance of life and the earth around him
he will always be performing "art."

Native American Saying

If you care about quality communication between people, if you are
willing to take a risk in order to create, if you are willing to be open,
flexible, vulnerable and experimental, you can successfully lead an
ACTING UP! drama group. No other requirements are necessary.

The ACTING UP! process does not require a specialized theatre
background. In fact, we have discovered the more openly you
approach your drama group workshop, the more successful you can
be. You are one voice who applauds and directs. You applaud by
encouraging each person to open up, take a risk, be a "ham", laughing
with the humor, empathizing with the recognition of difficult or
painful moments, and maintaining a supportive atmosphere in which
the ACTING UP! process may proceed. Your belief in the successful
growth and fulfillment of personal goals is important to the members
of your group.

It is fine if you are a person with a theatre background, but don't fall
into limiting yourself in the leadership role only if you are a theatre
professional. It is more important that the leader exhibit a humane
attitude. ACTING UP! requires above all a willingness to take a risk
and the desire to make discoveries about themselves through drama.

We have realized that in working with dramatic activities for older adults certain important needs have emerged directly from the group. Thus, we suggest the following leadership skills which are specifically designed for the leader of a drama workshop for older adults.

LISTEN TO THE TOTAL PERSON/ENCOURAGE THE MEMBERS TO BE ACTIVE LISTENERS

Learn to validate each other by listening with interest. Elders often feel as if they are invisible people in our society. Try to hear what they are communicating. In order to do this, you must listen to all forms of expression beyond words. Listen to what is being said through gestures, tone of voice and all the subtleties of body language.

As leader you become the group's therapist, its mother, its daughter, its best friend, its leader. You will often find it necessary to change roles according to its needs.

Listen and encourage ideas from the players in the group—ask what they want to accomplish. They want to be seen and heard. They are up there on stage to be recognized, to be seen as valuable, to feel that "I COUNT."

TOUCH IS A FORM OF LISTENING

Hugging a person when he needs a hug, holding hands for support or just a touch on the shoulder validates that person as important to you and to the group. Remember the saying, "You should pat yourself on the back for that!" It is a good idea not only to say, but do as well. Ashley Montague in his book entitled, *Touching, The Human Significance of Skin*, explains; "For human beings, tactile stimulation is of fundamental importance for the development of healthy emotional and affective relationships."

Often through habits of isolation, feeling alienated from the mainstream of society, and even in fear of their own sexuality, older adults in our society are "touch deprived." Your group will develop more positive attitudes, when they are given "touch support" and validation. Once the members see that it is OK for you to reach out, they will follow your lead and relax in this giving, supportive atmosphere.

CREATE A STRONG BASE FOR EACH ACTIVITY

When introducing a new activity to the group develop it as completely as possible yourself, demonstrating the new skills. Open yourself up to questions and comments so you know members understand completely what is to be done.

You may explain verbally, but in order for the "players" (the term we use to describe the participants of the group) to be sure of your meaning you must give an active demonstration. A new concept is easier to grasp if they can see the exercise in action. When the activity involves sharing autobiographical material, be ready to share your own experiences, joys, problems and frustrations.

SUPPORT AND VALIDATE AT EVERY STEP

A primary goal should be to aid the participants in better understanding themselves and the world in which they live, thereby leading to a deeper examination of the possibilities for living their lives.

In a workshop with Kenneth Koch, who edited, *I Never Told Anybody*, a leader asked, "Shouldn't you critique all along the way from beginning to end?" Mr. Koch replied with this analogy, "When you plant a garden and you see the first signs of growth, do you immediately prune them back or do you let them grow?" Everyone needs support and caring. When you are discovering something new it is important to know that any growth, no matter how small, is important. Criticism cuts back growth and sometimes diminishes it altogether.

Support is the nurturing base for growth and learning. Every group has its own unique personality, its own synergy. With a group of friends you can create a safe place for risk-taking. Establishing this safety is crucial to the group's creative endeavors. People explore and try new things when they feel safe with the people around them.

LEARN TO WORK WITH WHAT YOU HAVE

As a leader you will find there is no direct path to follow. You will want to be flexible and learn the art of taking side trips. Adaptation and flexibility mean learning to work with what you have. If you had planned to work toward a series of improvisational scenes for performance, and the group is more interested in oral literature and story-telling, follow the group's lead. Your own growth and fulfillment as a leader will benefit most from those unexpected moments and products that grow out of the members' interaction.

Maybe your group will go further than your expectations and maybe they won't go as far. The popular method so often used of approaching older people in the same way as children is a demeaning and completely inappropriate response. Remember that the older adults in your group are wise and authentic people with the courage to tell their real stories—presenting themselves as they are. When interacting with an audience, the charm and beauty of the performance comes across the "footlights" through the players' willingness to share something of themselves. This becomes much more important than a slick, polished performance.

THE VALUE OF HUMOR

We encourage laughter, a sense of humor, and the delight of discovery. We know that a human being's ability to laugh and appreciate humorous material is a valid indicator of his state of health. You will want to use the "language of exploration" rather than "the language of instruction." You now have become a model for "opening up"— not a judge. Having a sense of fun is an important asset for any leader. Have fun *with* the members of the group. If you can laugh with them it gives instant positive feedback and reinforces their positive self-images.

Individuals draw security and support from the group. Once the participants feel validated, they can be led into expressing deeper and more intense feelings. The valuable tool of humor is used by all people in order to survive. If part of your group's plans are to make dramatic statements on the myths of ageism and stereotyping, humor is one of the most effective teachers for audiences of all ages.

We have discovered for our ACTING UP! performances that a humorous presentation expresses complex ideas in a way people can understand. We believe that it is more fun and you can effectively deal with serious issues in a humorous manner. To the actors, laughter and applause of an appreciative audience are tremendous rewards.

TAKE A PIECE AS FAR AS POSSIBLE

Growth stops when risk-taking ends. Drama isn't just fun and games; it is also being moved to tears by sadness or joy, whether it's your own or someone else's. It is a positive form of catharsis; letting go of the emotion, giving it full release, dignity of conclusion and personal closure. No authentic emotion, creatively shared within a supportive group, is dangerous.

Although the scene should be allowed to develop without too much interference, there will be times when you, as leader, need to redirect the action to give the participants a new perspective on what is possible. Direct the conflict or problem to a resolution, if you can. Do not stop it in the middle because it is temporarily uncomfortable emotionally. This inhibits creative problem-solving. If the players hold back their emotions, their creative efforts tend to be suffocated rather than freed.

A woman brought a locket to class as a part of an activity. As she told the group about her locket, she began to cry. At first the other members reacted with nervous concern. But when we carried the story further, we discovered that she was relieved. It was the first time she had been able to talk about her late husband in fifteen years. Leadership means believing in the individual member's ability to deal with serious and problem topics without editing for her or being overprotective.

RECAPTURING THE HIGHS

At the end of each activity the players need to evaluate what has taken place. They should admire what went well, then review other possibilities or outcomes of the activity just performed, and try out or replay the group's variations or solutions to the activity, if appropriate.

To focus on the highs, you look at the positive elements of each activity. This helps you to know how well the group is progressing and stimulates the group to develop its own critical skills. Some questions for "Recapturing the Highs" are:

What moment in the scene or activity did you remember the most? Why? (It can be a piece of dialogue, a piece of action, or a non-verbal response from one player to another.)

Were you in any way affected by the scene or activity? How?

What contributed to your particular feeling?

Was there any evidence of "give and take" (talking and listening) in the scene or activity? Where?

If you have seen the players perform before, how did they grow in their performance skills?

Recapturing the high moments gives you an understanding of the group's best qualities and the areas needing improvement. The purpose of ACTING UP! is not to produce polished actors, but to point the way to self-discovery and awareness. *The performance is secondary to the actual process of the group as a learning-growing platform.*

TAKING CARE OF YOUR OWN NEEDS FOR FULFILLMENT AS A LEADER

Once you come to an understanding of what you are willing to give to the group, communicate your expectations to the group, eliciting their expectations as well. Deal in specifics of time, place, energy and commitment. Spell out, in small steps, the ground rules and get their agreement—their commitment to try.

You can build a support system for yourself within the group by asking for volunteers. If necessary, find another person to assist you in your duties. When the group needs support from within, help the members to develop it among themselves. This is especially important when illness or death arises. Because you listen to the group—it is important to find an outside person to listen to you. Do not be rushed into a performance by external requirements—allow yourself time to truly enjoy your experience.

ABOUT THIS BOOK

It is important to remember that taking activities directly from a book rarely guarantees success. Creative leaders will find that most of the activities in this book are adaptable for people with physical, mental or emotional handicaps. We strongly suggest that you experiment with developing your own variations to meet the needs and interests of your special group of players. The potential to be creative and imaginative is within all of us. We feel that the responsibility of the leader is to provide a nurturing environment in which the group can find its own unique rhythm. Drama is not something to be imposed upon a group, but a process to be developed and shared.

This book has been designed so that it can be used in a number of different ways. Stage One - "A Dramatic Change: Recovering Personal Stories," may be used in preparation for further (improvisation and performance) activities, or may be used as the basis for workshops that do not expand beyond the (less physically active) oral history, creative writing and storytelling stages. Groups which prefer to focus upon personal, community or regional oral history-gathering and recording techniques may find this chapter effective in capturing and documenting personal history and family folklore for written or spoken communication to other community groups. Where limiting physical activity is a concern, workshops may be devoted to stimulating verbal communication and shaping well-told or written stories and poetry.

Stage Two - "Act Your Age!" will be of interest both to groups who prefer active theatre improvisation and those preparing for performances. Stage Two is complete within itself, and if your group would rather not be concerned with a performance, an energetic series of workshops may be built around this section. If your group wishes to develop an original idea into a performance piece or wants to mount a published play, both Stage Two and Stage Three offer useful series of actors' warm-up activities which will enhance rehearsals.

Stage Three - "To Perform or Not to Perform" utilizes more advanced improvisational techniques and suggestions for developing original material into performance.

The choice to perform is an important one which you will want to discuss at length with the members of your group. Each stage and each activity offers the members a sense of closure and accomplishment. Every theatre game and improvisation should be approached as a performance. Thus, Stage Three need not lead to a formal performance, but can develop into mini-presentations during each meeting for members of the workshop.

You will find that many activities in each of the three stages build upon the previous section, repeat, intertwine and expand. The warm-up activities in each stage may be repeated as often as you choose. When you discover a drama activity to which your group especially responds, repeat it, follow up with suggested variations from the text, or collaborate on developing your group's own versions of the successful activity. Theatre improvisations are spontaneous and synergistic creations. Although they may eventually be scripted and rehearsed, they can also be repeated with slight changes and remain ever-new and vital.

The techniques of creative dramatics and improvised scenes serve other important purposes. They require no memorization. There is no "right" or "wrong" way to perform them. They draw naturally on autobiographical material and fantasy. They are a great stimulus for playwriting collaborations. They can be developed around contemporary concerns of importance about which the members of your group would like to make a statement. Improvisation encourages "thinking on your feet," immediate communication and the art of "give and take" between actors. Because improvisational techniques are egalitarian in form, they discourage the "star system" and encourage participation by all the actors. With every improvisation each ACTING UP! member has the opportunity to investigate new and challenging characters and dramatic situations.

Finally, the fact is that there are few vital, strong and meaningful parts or plays written for actors over the age of sixty. Improvisation assists ACTING UP! players to select and guide their own interests and aesthetic tastes. It allows them to develop, write, act in, and direct their personal creative statements for performances within the workshop group, or for communication to audiences of all ages.

> Youth is a work of nature
> Old age is a work of art.
> Anonymous

19

STAGE I - A DRAMATIC CHANGE: RECOVERING PERSONAL STORIES

It is only necessary to conceive the idea and allow for the experience to begin.

Brugh Joy

I can take any empty space and call it a bare stage. A man walks across this space whilst someone else is watching him, and this is all that is needed for an act of theatre to be engaged.

Peter Brook, The Empty Space

THE STAGE

Any space can become a stage. As long as we are willing to see that space as special, transformed in the way we choose, we can create a stage. If the location you will be using for your meetings is already familiar to your group as being used for purposes other than theatre (as it was for our group) you will need to find ways to transform it. Use a raised speakers platform, or make signs announcing your stage space.

After identifying this special space, it is wise to use this area only for work that will lead toward dramatic vignettes and storytelling experiences, thus making this area a symbolic space that means "stage" to your players. For our first two meetings we did not use the stage, although we discussed its importance and use in the near future. Instead, we sat in a circle, so that personal communication could grow easily and comfortably on a level that was familiar to the members of the group.

INTRODUCTION DUOS

It is difficult to listen to others introduce themselves one by one while you are trying frantically to think of what to say when your turn arrives. It is also difficult to assemble the interesting details about ourselves which will let others know us as unique and individual. We are trained to be humble, private, and subdued in our self-descriptions. The *Introduction Duo* allows us to pay close attention to others, and frees us from describing ourselves in ways gauged to win others' acceptance.

SETTING THE STAGE

Divide the group into pairs, encouraging the players to choose a partner whom they don't know. (The leader, too, should be part of an *Introduction Duo*.) Ask the players what things they would like to know most about their partners, for example:

What makes you laugh? Why?

What do you love most? Why?

What makes you angry? Why?

What is the most amazing thing that ever happened to you?

What are you afraid of?

What was your most daring undertaking?

What are you proud of in your life?

What is the central challenge in your life right now?

Are you the person you thought you would be? Why?

What is special about you?

What is your most outrageous fantasy?

What do you want people to know about you that isn't readily apparent?

What are your most prized talents or areas of expertise?

After the group has developed a number of suggestions that reach beyond superficial questions to those which can assist in recognizing more meaningful individual qualities, write the suggestions on a blackboard or large piece of paper for easy reference.

Partners meet together and divide time equally. They cover as many of the suggested questions as they wish, adding appropriate questions along the way.

Each member is responsible to introduce his or her partner to the rest of the group. In this activity each partner must listen closely, acting as a thoughtful interviewer with the sole purpose of capturing what is special about his partner for presentation to the rest of the group. *Listening with interest is the key to this activity.* Being a responsible representative for another person encourages quality listening which will form the basis for the group's future work as an ensemble.

Even if the members of your group believe that they know one another quite well, this experience will reveal that there are endless, fascinating qualities to be discovered about each other. You have encouraged the members to go beyond standard social responses. They will begin moving gracefully toward the recognition of one another as interesting and unpredictable individuals with wonderfully unique lives, needs and opinions which are worth communicating to others.

After the Duos have spent sufficient time getting to know one another return to the circle to begin introductions. A good way to begin presenting your partner is with a short descriptive character statement. These are several openings from our *Introduction Duos:*

> "This is Shirley. She describes herself as an independent spirit who has been grounded for years and is just waiting for the inspiration to take off...."

> "Meet Ben who came to the group because he's tired of the 3:30 afternoon movies, and he hopes this will be more interesting than watching T.V....."

POINTS TO REMEMBER

One of the hurdles for people of all ages to overcome is the feeling that their personal experiences and life stories are not unique and could not, therefore, be interesting to others. Because so much of the ACTING UP! process involves translating autobiographical material to written story-telling and improvisational performance techniques, it is important, from the first exchanges of personal stories, that the group members be supported and validated for their shared experiences. These are the initial steps toward theatre and should be treated as such, not with critiques on style, performance and method, but with discussions of successful points and discoveries.

RECAPTURING THE HIGHS

After the introductions ask each member of the group how it felt to be interviewed and presented to the others through his or her partner:

What did you enjoy?

How did you feel about becoming a "character" in your own story?

Did your partner interpret the facts correctly?

Did she listen carefully and remember the important points?

What was the easiest question to answer? The hardest? Why?

What did your interviewer do to make you feel comfortable?

What did you enjoy about interviewing your partner?

What was the easiest question to ask? The most difficult? Why?

What question was most revealing?

What brought the most humorous response?

Do you feel that you have had the opportunity to get to know your partner in a unique way?

Explain to the group that through this activity they have experienced some of the initial steps that a playwright follows when she is developing a character for the stage. She asks questions of the characters she is forming in her imagination; although most of them are drawn from personal stories she has experienced or has been told. It has been said that the art of theatre is nothing more than relationships and shared experiences. Good theatre is the ordered telling of personal stories for universal appeal.

The following activities in the ACTING UP! process are based on bringing forth and fashioning personal moments into improvisations and dramatic vignettes.

LET'S TALK ABOUT IT

In our first meetings five years ago we worked carefully at building a comfortable and candid relationship among the members that would help us consider and find solutions to some of the concerns facing this unique group.

After several weeks of introductions and casual discussions we began to consider some of the most interesting ideas, those that spoke to all of us, as material to be developed for the future. Several of the players began working on brief script outlines, jotting down the important points we had considered in our discussion sessions on the myths of aging. Soon they had begun collaborating on possible dramatic protrayals of these concerns.

Under the direction of one of the players, we considered some of the important transition stages in life in which we make the statement "I wish I were older because...." (See appendix for "Premiere Performance of ACTING UP!") This vignette spoke to audiences of all ages and became the finale of our first performances. It is still used (in an abbreviated version) by the present ACTING UP! troupe.

Let's Talk About It sessions became an important part of every meeting. Each week we discussed the events of that day's meeting and encouraged candor and full participation in all decisions made by the group. In this way we began to build a strong ensemble spirit that gave the members confidence as individuals. Through this shared validation we began to introduce new activities that would challenge more and more of each individual's abilities while offering group support for risk-taking steps to come.

INVESTED OBJECTS

In theatre the term *Invested Object* is used to describe a hand-prop or set piece in which a particular character has invested a great deal of personal meaning. This object often tells us about the character's past, his personal response to the world around him and indicates what he holds dear about his life.

For the members of ACTING UP! an *Invested Object* can be a strong stimulus for the development of writing personal histories, family folklore and group storytelling.

LEADER PREPARATION

Ask the members of the group to bring transportable objects which remind them of a specific time in their lives, a special person or meaningful situation in which they received or found their object. All of us have a special keepsake which we carry in our pocket, purse, keep in a treasured box or wear because it makes us feel most in touch with ourselves and an important part of our lives.

Ask the members to think about those events which surround the discovery or purchase of the object. If it is an heirloom or keepsake from an important person, why is this object a special reminder of that individual?

SETTING THE SCENE

Bring an important object of your own with which to stimulate the groups thinking over the next week. Spend time visualizing the events surrounding your discovery of that keepsake and prepare a personal story which involves the feelings and emotions evoked by your invested object.

As we hold and share the object with the rest of the group, we feel as if we have taken the stage to tell about an old friend. We are responsible only for telling a story which we know, and which has particular meaning for us.

This is a safe way to begin storytelling within the group. You may also want to bring various small objects and pass them around, asking the group to create a fictional story about the person to whom the object belongs, and the events surrounding it. Why is this object important? What does it mean to the character you are creating in your collaborative story? What does this invested object symbolize about our character and her life? What do we know about the inner feelings of our character through her choice of this prized possession? What was her life like before she found or was given her keepsake? How did the object change her life? To whom will she pass on this possession, and what will she say when she does so?

POINTS TO REMEMBER

Encourage members to share personal feelings about an object, no matter how plain, or unusual it might be. Shirley Helfand brought a pair of her mother's flannel teddies (warm bloomers) which she had kept since the Depression. After some initial laughter, she told us a very moving story. The Depression had been tough for the family. At times there was no heat and little food. Her mother had made these warm teddies for herself one day after bundling the children off to school. In them she was able to go on about her chores without stoking the fire until the children came home at night, and still wear the dignified skirts and dresses which she felt a woman must maintain even in hard times. The woman telling the story realized her mother's struggle. She kept the teddies in a special drawer to remind her of her mother's courage and dignity.

Tom Burns brought an old pocket knife he had received as a boy from a favorite aunt. To him it symbolized the first moment that he was recognized as a responsible, independent person. He carried the pocket knife with him at all times, through childhood, World War II, business life, and now to help him feel lucky on the golf course. His knife was an especially provocative stimulus because it set off a cycle of stories about unusual members of his family, larger-than-life characters who had influenced him.

These first storytellings are important to you and the group. They allow participants to perform "on-stage" using familiar and non-threatening props to stimulate memory and imagination. The words are their own, and no other character is on stage with them. The memories and images evoked by the *invested objects* lead to poetry and fiction writing activities, and to the development of possible characters and plots for future improvised scenes and collaborative playwriting activities. Most important, they allow you and the rest of the group to reveal special moments and meaningful feelings from your lives within a supportive, comfortable atmosphere.

As a leader, you will find that allowing the members of the group an opportunity to begin to truly know you is as important as your discovery of each of them as unique individuals.

WHO AM I? COLLAGE

Everyone's life can be seen as a series of layers, textures, colors, shapes and forms. If we were to select a moment from our lives and create a collage from "found" objects readily available to us which makes a statement about who we are right now, we could see ourselves captured visually as a work of art. The *Who Am I? Collage* allows us free reign to select from the flotsam and jetsam of our lives—scrapbooks, junk-drawers and printed materials—to fashion a multi-faceted picture of ourselves.

LEADER PREPARATION

Prepare your own *Who Am I? Collage* from interesting clippings from newspapers, magazines, pieces of cloth, wood, found objects, photos, etc. Select each piece for visual interest. Give yourself plenty of time to collect materials for your collage. By not limiting the time, you will react more spontaneously to those things in your environment which you identify with yourself.

Glue, paint, draw and staple, combining the pieces in an old box, drawer, or on a piece of cardboard or wood. You can use a three dimensional "frame" to enclose your work, or choose an object like a tennis racquet, hat, poncho or shirt to broaden your choice of a "canvas." (Many Native Americans decorated shields, clothing and banners with emblems which indicated, through illustrated stories and adventures from their lives, who the bearers were.) Plan an informal explanation of the choices you made and the meaning each piece of the collage has for you. Share your *Who Am I? Collage* with the group and listen to members' responses to your work.

Guide the group through the process of creating your collage. Emphasize spontaneity in discovering and assembling pieces. In a throw-away culture we all have endless textures, colors and varieties of objects squirreled away that would make interesting visual pieces. You might want to think of these collages as modern day personal totems, parts of our life stories captured in visual imagery.

The meanings that the collages had for their creators was as stimulating as the collages themselves. Spontaneous visual representations of ourselves are exciting to both the artist and the viewer. We learn about our inner attitudes toward our lives, and our choices for outward expression of ourselves through this activity. Secret talents, political statements, varied interests, personal goals are among the many perceptions revealed through the *Who Am I? Collage.*

YOGA AND BODY DYNAMICS

It is important for you and your group to develop your own exercise routine for use before rehearsals and performances. With all of the excellent books on yoga and body dynamics available, we do not feel that it is necessary to concentrate on detailed discussions of physical warm-ups. You will find the time well-spent if you experiment with different exercise routines which best suit the needs and capacities of your group. We found that Gay Luce's excellent book, *Your Second Life* (see Bibliography), was an excellent source for warm-up, stretching and flexibility exercises. We particularly appreciated her gentle, yet persistent, instruction that a more limber, relaxed body and proper

approach to breathing are of utmost importance to physical, emotional and spiritual well-being. We strongly suggest that you discover a series of three to five exercises which the members of your group come to value as a daily at-home breathing-stretching-warm-up routine.

We used three basic yoga warm-ups, which we changed and adapted to the needs of the group. These warm-ups were based on traditional postures found in almost any basic Hatha yoga book and have been used consistently before rehearsals and performances by the ACTING UP! troupe. We begin our exercises with the *Cosmic Wheel*, a limbering, stretching series of fluid movements for the waist, back and upper body. Next, we perform an abbreviated version of the *Sun Salutation* which stretches the entire torso, allows players to bend and "hang" gently from the waist, and to rid themselves of physical tension by "centering" their energy in a calm and meditative manner.

Finally, we practice a simplified form of *Alternate Nostril Breathing* which clears our heads, sends fresh oxygen supplies to the brain, stimulates the creative thought processes and offers a powerful energy boost before beginning a rehearsal or performance.

Throughout our years together we have also experimented with adaptations of *T'ai Chi* movements as well as jogging in place, creative forms of tag and other improvised games and sports activities. A number of these warm-up exercises have become part of the performance, and often involve audience participation. It seems that the more eclectic the exercise ritual, the more interesting and challenging it is for us, even after numerous repetitions. Also, you will discover, as we did, that most simple yoga routines and many other body dynamics exercises can be adapted for use by players with various handicapping conditions. We have introduced our exercise regimen in Veterans Administration hospitals, nursing homes and with individuals in walkers and wheel chairs.

EMOTIONAL SYMPHONY

Now that the group is comfortable with expressing itself verbally, and has begun tapping its autobiographical materials which will eventually lead to oral history tellings and writings, introduce a simple theatre game. This is your opportunity to test the response of your group's interest in advancing beyond discussion and the first stages of storytelling. The *Emotional Symphony* is a vocal warm-up adapted from Viola Spolin's theatre game techniques which allows the players to experiment with sound improvisations. In addition, they will begin responding to audience suggestions.

SETTING THE STAGE

Three to six actors take places on stage. Ask the rest of the group for emotions to suggest to each performer. Explain that the performers are a unique and sophisticated group of artists who play special instruments—the vocal chords. Each player is given an emotion suggested by the group (anger, lust, the willies, horror, nervousness—the more creative the better). She "plays" that emotion by making a nonverbal sound which illustrates it (grr! whew!, ahhh!).

After all of the performers have practiced their emotion-sounds the "Choral Director" (the leader) explains his directing technique. By pointing to each player when it is her turn to perform—cutting off sounds in mid-vocalization, "playing" louder, softer, faster, slower, duets, trios and solos—the director conducts the *Emotional Symphony*.

This improvisation provides an exciting release for inhibitions and tension, and warms up the voice and upper body through active involvement. You can repeat this activity with different performers, new choral directors and new suggestions for emotions. The performers concentrate on the directions of the conductor, responding immediately to directions. This is a fine exercise for introducing ensemble acting and "focusing" attention.

VARIATIONS

1. When the players are sufficiently warmed-up you can introduce nonsense words, phrases or proverbs to be performed by the *Emotional Symphony* members. Each phrase should be spoken with a suggested emotion. For example, one could speak angrily, "A stitch in time saves nine," or passionately, "Just give me a turkey sandwich and hold the mayo." Each player speaks the same phrase, but with her own emotion. Conduct these *Symphonies* as you did the first one.

2. The *Natural Sounds Symphony* variation begins with a chorus of six or more players selecting a place in nature—midwestern front yard, Florida swamp, Colorado mountain stream, vegetable garden, Sahara Desert. The audience selects a site, time of day and a season. (It should be understood that these are organic, natural sites, and not the sounds, themselves.) For example, for a midwestern garden early in the morning at midsummer, sound creators might be oak trees catching soft wind, robins searching for worms, bees buzzing, worms tunneling in roots, roosters crowing, dogs barking in the distance, or rabbits chewing lettuce leaves. Once the *Natural Sounds Symphony* has warmed up the players, direct them as you did in the *Emotional Symphony*. As the director you may sequence the sounds as they happen in nature.

FAVORITE PERSON INTERVIEW

Now that the players have had an opportunity to informally inter-view one another in the *Introduction Duos,* have experienced brief storytelling activities in the *Invested Object,* and have shared a group improvisation in the *Emotional Symphony,* they are ready for a more sophisticated theatre game which combines all of these techniques. *Favorite Person Interview* is a dynamic way to experiment with stage character development, while investigating personal philosophies and interests through role-playing. This activity may be handled as a discussion stimulus where players simply talk about their favorite person, or it can lead to an active dramatic representation with props, a simple set and supporting characters. Depending upon your group's needs and interests, you can tailor this experience as an active perform-ance for the rest of the group, or as a personal experience to be undertaken privately by each member.

LEADER PREPARATION

Throughout our lives we have come to admire special individuals from history, literature, science and other fields who represent for us the accomplishments of a life successfully lived. Often these heroes and heroines are larger-than-life characters, the subject of biography, myth and legend. We may even find that they have served as secret models, guides or inner counselors for decisions we make in our lives. They embody important traits such as courage, dignity, innovation and striving for a unique view of the world upon which their individual characters have made a mark. They are the symbols of our personal potential.

Select a favorite person from history or literature to whom you would like to speak. How would you introduce this character to others? Why has she been important to you? What qualities do you most admire in your favorite person? How has the example he set guided you at various points in your life? After you have considered your reason for selecting your favorite person, prepare a list of inter-view questions to ask him or her. Include in this list any questions for which you might want guidance in your own life, e.g., who were your heroes when you were young? How do you deal with fame? Did you ever have doubts about who you are and what you do?

SETTING THE STAGE

Place two chairs on stage. In one chair, seat your imaginary favorite person. The interviewer sits in the other chair. In this role-playing activity the interviewer speaks to the empty chair as if it were her favorite person. First, the favorite person is introduced to the rest of the players as a special friend of the interviewer. Then the interviewer makes comments directly to the favorite person, explaining to him why he has been an important model to her. She asks him several questions which pertain to personal questions or goals she is considering in her own life. How does he deal with similar concerns in his life? What advice would he give her, based upon his own personal experience?

ROLE-REVERSAL

The interviewer now switches chairs and becomes her favorite person. We found that one or two pieces of costume, an *invested object* or hand prop help represent the character more easily. Louis Armstrong had his large white handkerchief and a horn, Thomas Jefferson, his quill pen and Albert Einstein, his pipe and baggy sweater. The painter, Georgia O'Keefe, dressed in black and brought along a paint brush and a large soup-bone to represent her skull and antler paintings. Merlin wore a hooded sweater and carried a rubber frog for casting quick spells and making potions, and so on. Getting into character is not difficult once the importance of switching chairs is established, and the favorite person has been asked some interesting questions about his or her life and philosophy.

The advice that the favorite person gives to the interviewer, now represented by the empty chair, can prove to be quite meaningful to the player creating the role. To the amazement of our players, most of the personal advice asked of the favorite person was answered by workable solutions. A woman who had thought about painting for many years, but had not found the time nor the confidence to begin, told herself with typical Georgia O'Keefe directness: "Don't listen to anyone but yourself. Begin painting the way I did by investigating black and white, until you feel you are ready to use color. And pay no attention to the voices that try to stop you. I created some of my greatest works in my sixties after they said I had no more to give!" Merlin told his interviewer that it was time to believe in a little personal magic, to trust his intuition and follow whatever notion he had in mind. "After all," said Merlin, "I am over one thousand years young, if my addition is correct, and look at me—still going strong!" Merlin then cast a spell on his interviewer, making him the greatest ballroom dancer around. The actor listened, thought about it, went to work for several years, and today this ACTING UP! member is teaching ballroom dancing at community centers throughout Chicago.

The *Favorite Person Interview* can be adapted to your group's interests in a number of different ways. You can ask the players to write a dialogue of their interview by playing both roles on paper. Future scripts can be drawn from these dialogues, or they can be kept as personal references. The dialogues can include important considerations, both personal and universal. The members of your group may want to interview their favorite person concerning their attitudes toward myths of aging, and the way they dealt with these prejudices.

We encouraged strong individual connections with favorite persons we selected. We came to see them as inner guides and teachers who can consult with us and give advice concerning many of our personal decisions. We also discovered that we no longer needed to write out our dialogues. After we had created our favorite person characters on paper and on stage, we found it comfortable to hold these dialogues in our imaginations whenever we felt we could benefit from the favorite person's counsel.

VARIATIONS

You may want to expand the *Favorite Person Interviews* into press conferences. In this variation other players interview the favorite person as a panel of journalists, scientists, doctors or other special group. You can create an Expert Speakers' Bureau in which the Favorite Persons address the audience as after-dinner speakers, commenting on their unique lives and personal philosophies.

We encourage this form of role-playing in many of our intergenerational forums with high school and college students. Role-reversals allowed the younger participants to experience the myths and prejudices of ageism through the eyes of their elders. The older actors discovered how thoughtful and open-minded many of their personal attitudes were when they took the roles of teenagers and young adults.

SENSORY EXERCISES

"The body knows long before the mind recognizes."
Yaqui Native American Saying

Our senses—touch, smell, taste, sight and hearing—bring us information about the world. As we get older we may begin to shut down these pathways to perception, believing in the myth that they are no longer operational. Even though one or two of the senses may not be as sharp, we can continually cultivate their use. The many senses are not equally balanced in terms of stimuli input. We respond much more to sight than to the other senses, and the older adult uses sight often to the exclusion of the other senses in making decisions concerning her body and the environment. Sight is important, but the other senses should not be neglected. Each contributes to our understanding of the world. Sensory stimulation can help to sharpen receptivity to the world around us. We have created some exercises to heighten the group's sense-awareness, which will help each person develop his ability to form a mental picture from the sensory experience. Imagination is central to all theatre games and the senses provide stimuli that generate imaginative thought and action. *Remember throughout these activities that attention to specific and concrete detail is important.*

TOUCH I

Divide the group into pairs to do the "blind walk." The players, deprived of sight, use their other senses—especially touch and hearing—to explore the environment. One player closes her eyes and keeps them closed (a blindfold can be used, but it isn't necessary). The other player leads, undertaking full responsibility for his "sightless" partner. The leader does not touch the partner in any way but gives direction by voice, and the group leader may need to demonstrate the kinds of directions needed, for example, "three steps down, reach to the right for the railing, two steps to your right...." The partner does not talk much or ask questions, but is a receptor to the non-visual stimuli bombarding her. Each partner can have fifteen to thirty minutes, and the walk can cover both inside and outside environments. Members should be encouraged to explore different sensations, water fountains, trees, grass, sand, glass doors, unusual textures. When the activity is over, discuss the experience. Which senses were more vivid? Were you able to "trust" your partner? What did you discover about yourself? What did you learn about your body and its way of speaking to you in its subtle and wise voices? Describe how these "voices" spoke through your senses and all your body parts.

TOUCH II

Half the members of the group close their eyes (blindfolds can be used). Match each of these people with a seeing partner. The "sightless" person touches the seeing partner's hands, back and face. The seeing players then move around the room. At this point the first players take off their blindfolds and try, with their eyes open, to identify their partner.

TEXTURES

Sit in a circle and have the players close their eyes (blindfolds may be used). Pass around a variety of textured objects. Through the sense of touch (and smell) the players try to identify the objects.

Some examples are: feather, silk scarf, sandpaper, burlap, fur collar, nylon stocking, metal cup. These textures will evoke graphic images in the minds of the players. Have them describe the textures, for example: scratchy, smooth, rough, cold, slimy. With textures in mind, the players create characters. For example: from the word smooth, a used car salesman might be created; from the word scratchy, a tired grouchy maid might be created.

SMELL

Sit in a circle and pass around small bags or containers, each with a different herb, spice or fruit. Each player determines what the particular smell is and describes associations the smell conjures up in his mind. Again, encourage the players to be *precise, concrete* and *specific* as they describe the details of their images.

The smells can be unpleasant as well as pleasant. One player, when smelling a chicken bullion cube, was reminded of holiday times in Russia, family gatherings and the warm time she had as a child. Characters can also be conjured up from smells. From the sharp, pungent, sour smell of vinegar you can conjure up a miserly prudish clerk; the sweet, light, delicate smell of perfume may conjure up a young Tahitian woman gathering Hibiscus blossoms in her skirt.

TASTE

Organize a pot luck lunch or dinner for which everyone brings something different to eat. Have people describe the taste and their associations. The players describe the differences in the tastes and textures: nutty tasting, bland, exciting, spicy. Look for evocative words not normally used when describing tastes: ornate, respectable, green and shivery.

Describe the scene and location evoked by these smells and tastes. What character might you be if you were in the taste-smell sensory scene you just described? Include as much detail as possible. (The smell and taste of radishes might take you to a Russian garden in the 1880's, or you might become a rabbit nibbling at radishes in a garden. With the taste of hot peppers, you might be in the hot sun of Acapulco.)

SIGHT

Pair off and have the players look closely at their partners. The players turn around, back-to-back. One of the players changes five things on her body (untie a shoelace, put glasses away, part hair on different side). The players face each other again, and then must guess what five things are different. Switch to the other person so that every player gets a chance to change and to guess. The point of this exercise is to enhance concentration, close observation, and fine discrimination.

SENSE ORIENTATION

All the players walk around the room, observing closely what objects and colors are in the room. With their eyes closed, the leader calls out a color or object in the room and everyone points as fast as possible to the color or object. The players must have a sense of orientation in the room to be able to figure out where the object is in relation to where they are now.

OBJECT RECALL

Bring in a tray with a variety of different objects. Everyone observes the objects; then take the tray away. See how many objects players can recall. This exercise helps players' awareness of both objects within the space and the empty spaces around them. Note the importance each individual places upon those objects most easily remembered. What connections or memories in our individual lives do the remembered objects evoke? Why do we remember the things we do?

SOUND AWARENESS

The players sit with their eyes closed and listen for as many sounds as possible in the space around them. Develop specific sound focus by having the players listen to distant sounds outside the building, outside the room, around their bodies. Listen to inner sounds, heart beating, breath filling lungs, blood rushing through veins, muscle twitches. Have the players open their eyes and talk about what they heard. Some players will hear only the basic sounds. Others will hear more subtle sounds such as the water dripping in the bathroom, the furnace switching on, a cough, footsteps, a train in the distance.

SOUND TAPE

Use a sound tape made up of a variety of sounds, such as an osterizer, telephone, crumpling a bag, door-bell ring, typewriter, running water. Players identify each sound and the imagery it conjures up.

For instance, running water may remind one player of a rapidly rushing river in the mountains of Colorado while it is associated with a troublesome toilet from childhood for another player. Be specific. Allow everyone enough time to verbalize fully-imagined scenes. One player created the following poem from images developed in working with the sense-imagery exercises:

Don't You Ever Tell
"Don't you tell anyone," my mother said
As we placed the bags of food
On the kitchen table.
The apples were red,
But not shiny;
The potatoes, bumpy and brown;
The sugar and rice and flour
Were as white as a dingy bedsheet.

"Don't you tell anyone," my mother said.
She needn't have worried.
My shame lay coiled
In the pit of my stomach;
I had no room for hunger anymore.
We put away cans and boxes of food;
We surely would not starve.

"Don't you tell anyone," my mother said,
And in the winter's cold kitchen,
My body was hot from the burning flame of
Guilt?
A nameless horror in our lives?
A fault we had
That must be hidden from the world?
What terrible deed had we committed?

"Don't you tell anyone," my mother said,
And I sensed her pain and despair.
We had, on that unforgettable day,
Accepted free food
From the City.

And I never told anyone.
But now, I've told you.

Birdell E. Provus, 1980

THE DRAMATIC ART OF STORYTELLING: HISTORY IS YOUR STORY

...we have a treasure-house of material, stored through these six thousand years, within reach of hand and imagination. As distributors we can do a fine piece of work, remembering always that to tell a story is not enough, remembering to honor what we tell, and to bring to the receptivity of the listener something of the universal appeal, the deep significance of folk-literature—to touch the heart that the head may understand.

Ruth Sawyer, *The Way of the Storyteller*

Oral storytelling is the one art form that is natural to all human beings. Storytelling is the first of all the written and performed arts and the foundation of modern drama. Why is oral history and the folk literature which surrounds it so important? With the advent of radio, television, movies and mass media which attempt to tell stories for us, the art of storytelling began to disappear. At the end of each generation, important personal histories are lost or forgotten—histories filled with the everyday events of life-celebrations, rituals, insight into political ideas, personal reactions to world-wide events, family relationships, ethnic heritage, religion, community and regional traditions and language, the unique view of the individual within a much larger world. Oral histories provide the vital connective tissue which brings world history to life. The dramatic art of storytelling allows us to communicate history as we have lived it.

TAKING A GUIDED IMAGERY TOUR

Ask the group to find relaxed positions in comfortable chairs, lying on the floor or with pillows propped against the walls. Begin the *Guided Imagery Tour* with simple relaxation exercises that work best for you. You may begin, as we did, with yoga-breathing exercises, concentrating on inhaling slowly and thinking of the most beautiful color of green you can imagine. While exhaling, think of tensions being released in the colors of dark gold or orange. Ask the players to look up to the spot where their "third eye" might be, while keeping

39

their eyes shut. (Several Native American and Australian aboriginal tribes believed that the "third eye" or the "dream-spirit eye" is at the center of the forehead, between our two physical eyes.) Tell the players that by concentrating on the images created by the "third eye" they will be able to "see" details and experience smells, sounds, colors, etc. in the personal *Guided Imagery Tour* upon which you are about to take them.

If further relaxation seems to be required, suggest that they are standing in front of a large old-fashioned trunk. They unlock the lid of the trunk and open it wide to receive, one by one, all of the worries, concerns and tensions of the day. Ask them to clearly visualize each of these concerns as they place it in the trunk. Now the trunk is closed and locked, and they may proceed on their imagery journey without considering these things again.

The following are only suggestions for the imagery tours upon which you may want to guide your group. We use this procedure before performing, before writing, or just to relax after a hectic day. Often we take five or ten minutes to wind-down in this way after rehearsals, reminding ourselves of what we learned and experienced that day in the workshop, and recapturing the highs as we are relaxing.

Guided Imagery Tours should be led slowly, and at a relaxed pace, for a period of fifteen minutes to one-half hour. Pause and give the players time to develop the details of their images. Don't try to speed through this experience, or include too many stimuli during one session. This experience takes repetition and practice both for you as guide, and for the players. Learning to tune out the noise and distractions of the every-day world is an art to be cultivated slowly. When you and your group have begun to accomplish this, you will be more in tune with the creative power of your autobiographical experiences and imaginings.

PERSONAL IMAGERY TOURS

A. Everyday Life and Family Rituals. Do you remember your first childhood home? Take a walk through that house or apartment and see, touch and smell all those things you know so well. Where was your special place for dreaming, thinking and getting away from the world? What are you doing? What can you see, hear, feel? Remember Christmas, Passover, Thanksgiving or other family gatherings? Remember when your grandparents and distant relatives all got together? You are there now. Everyone is sitting around the fire in the evening and stories are being told. There are stories about how your family came to this country, this region and this city. Focus on the everyday occurrences, how food was prepared, how you traveled from one place to another, what you did for recreation, the difference in education and types of jobs or crafts people prided themselves in. There are stories about your parents' and grandparents' childhoods, and your growing-up years, first jobs, how relatives met and married, stories of births, weddings, family celebrations and rituals. Are there any skeletons in the family closet? Any famous or notorious relatives or friends?

B. *Family Folklore, Superstitions, Myths, Home Remedies and Earth Wisdom.* How about good jokes on family members or friends? Maybe there are some whoppers and tall tales being told at this family gathering. Maybe there are ghost stories, stories of adventure and exploration, embarrassing stories, touching stories, joyous stories, humorous stories or tales of heroism and courage. Are there any myths passed down through your family—bedtime stories or creative explanations for why the world is the way it is?

How about good family and regional or ethnic home remedies for colds, arthritis, burns, the "miseries," plague, dropsy, chilblains, "complaints and problems of the gender," hiccups, consumption, black eyes, sprains, childbirth, fertility, broken hearts, unrequited love, hair growth or loss, etc? What superstitions were passed along in your neighborhood or from the old country? Remember how your relatives predicted changes in weather and their particular wisdom about nature, the earth and elements, how to plant and tend a fine truck garden, predict the size of a harvest, when a mare would foal, how to find water and how deep to dig the well?

C. *Being Aware of Storytelling "Styles," Settings and Specifics* Listen and *see* the stories being told as if you were experiencing them exactly as you did long ago. How are they being told? Who is telling them? Does the teller have any special accent, drawl or favorite sayings? What is the rhythm of the storyteller's words? Does he or she use characteristic gestures and facial expressions? How do you feel as you listen to the retelling of these stories or relive actual events from your own life? What was it like to live through a world war, the Depression, the dawning of the TV age and space travel? Remember the specifics and details. Look around the room in your mind and study everything there—the people, objects, the quality of the light, sounds, smells, etc. *Discover the most concrete and specific details.* For example, if you can hear a clock ticking in the "imagery" room, was it like an irregular heartbeat, a rusty insect chirp, water dripping

41

on tin? Reach for the precise details which make the story *yours*. Always remember, *no one knows what you know in the same way that you know it.*

After you have taken several *Guided Imagery Tours* together, begin focusing from the general historical framework of the lives of the people in your group to the specifics of their personal experiences. Because you have listened closely to the members of your group up to this point, you will have an idea of the important cultural, social, historical and community concerns and experiences which are most meaningful to them. Try to guide them toward particular key moments, personal experiences and memories which express their position in and view of the world. Think of yourself as an oral historian, a collector of personal stories which are important to future generations. The people in your group are storehouses of valuable memories and life-dramas. They have lived through some of the greatest changes in the history of civilization and they are the artistic creators and transmitters of those most magical forms of American literature—oral tradition, history, folklore and legend. Their lives and views deserve to be preserved and communicated.

Ask the players to write the memories that appeared. The purpose of *Guided Imagery Tours* is to stimulate memories and stories that are so clear and intensely felt that they must be communicated in a broader way, through writing and performance. After capturing the stories in a basic written plot, the urge to communicate them further by oral storytelling will be heightened.

Your group may want to further develop its folklore and oral histories through an expanded improvisation technique which we call *Magic Memories,* a form of story theatre (see Stage II). The members may want to write these stories complete with dialogue, setting, description and action. You may even want to go a step further to the develop a Readers' Theatre presentation of their work. Each of these activities heightens the reminiscences, allowing the players to capture and communicate their autobiographical material.

WRITTEN STORY OUTLINES

Take a few minutes and jot down five sentences which outline the story each would most like to tell. (Your group may wish to develop expanded creative writing pieces at this point. We found that the written histories, family folklore and local legends we gathered would

make a fine small magazine to be read and appreciated by local residents and historians and collected in the community library.)

PARTNER STORY PREPARATION

With a partner, tell *about* your story in just a minute or two. Now, sit and think about an introduction to your story; set the scene. Where was the story first told? Does the story take place in another time, a far-off place, or in your own lifetime? Who is telling the story? Or, who was involved in the dramatic situation or incident which you experienced? Is this a scary story, a romantic story, a heroic story or a touching story? "Set the stage" in your listener's imagination and help him prepare the proper mood for the story that is to follow.

Look at your list of five sentences which outline your story; make notes as to where you should build excitement, how you should describe the characters so that he can "see" them physically and immediately. Should you take different parts, change your voice or your physical position as you create different characters? Where does the climax of the story occur? How would you like to tell a short, clear ending?

PARTNER STORYTELLING REHEARSAL

In *Partner Storytelling Rehearsal,* tell your story to your partner as if he or she were the audience. Don't memorize. Storytelling should begin as a spontaneous art. Keep the stories to three to five minutes in length. This kind of formal storytelling is usually performed in a seated position, with the audience gathered close to the storyteller.

1. Remember to include a short, direct introduction.

2. Use natural gestures—no need to be overly-dramatic. Every storyteller develops his or her own unique style—be true to what is most comfortable for you.

3. Keep eye-contact with your partner. Storytelling is a shared, participatory art. Your partner is as involved as you, the storyteller, imagining in her own mind the world you create, and the characters and action which take place there. She should feel that this story is for her.

4. Use a voice which is expressive but *natural.* Practice varying pitch, rhythm and volume to create a sense of *real* life about events that are happening right now. Above all, make sure that your audience does not have to strain to hear you.

5. *Allow yourself to relax and enjoy.* The true art of storytelling involves a feeling of informality—even in the formal telling of tales. Now, switch with your partner and listen to his storytelling performance. You are now the coach. Help your partner develop the above good storytelling techniques.

DUO STORYTELLING

After the players have prepared stories and coached each other through several story developments and casual performances, you may want to expand the experience to include *Duo Storytelling.*

Duo Storytelling gives players the opportunity to perform with another storyteller and to practice the important "give and take" of ensemble acting. Divide players into small groups of three or four and ask one of the members in each group to begin telling a spontaneous story drawn straight from her imagination. Each time the leader calls out, "Change," the story must be picked up where it was left off by the next player and continued without breaking the flow of the telling. (Note: The most important point here is that each person listen carefully to the person who speaks before her and not concentrate on telling perfectly created stories. The story can then be continued in mid-sentence, each person responding with the very next word she thinks of to finish the thought left by the former teller.) When the players practice this kind of quick change response, they will be aware that their collaborative stories have a seamless quality, as if they were being told by a single multi-faced storyteller. It is this "seamless flow" that you and the players observe as you rehearse this activity.

After this exercise becomes comfortable for small groups, ask players to divide up into duos to begin developing couple storytellings. For this exercise you will need typed copies of short traditional folk or fairy tales (simply condense well-known tales into one-page fact sheets). Give each of the players a copy of the story and after they have read it, ask them to talk about the story to their partners, but not to tell their partners the entire story. When they are comfortable that each is clear on the basic points, characters and action of the story, ask one of the players to begin telling the story in a dramatic manner following the important points from *Partner Storytelling Rehearsal*. It is the second player's responsibility to take over the telling of the story when he feels that a different character's voice would be interesting, when there is a change in the action or when a description of setting, character or mood would add to the telling.

You may want to call out, "Change," at first, to get the duos moving. But eventually the natural exchange of telling, sharing the story and recognizing the points in the story which are enhanced by switching back and forth from teller to teller should become a comfortable experience for the players. You will want to remind the players not to discuss how they should perform, nor to carefully plan their telling exchanges. This should grow organically out of their work together. Eventually, a dramatic relationship between the two storytellers will evolve. This is an experience of great importance to the improvisation activities which follow in the next two stages of the book.

Next, give each storyteller a typed copy of personal stories written by the players. Ask the duo players to develop one of the personal, autobiographical stories into a performance, telling it in exactly the same way that they prepared the classic fairy or folk tale. After sufficient rehearsal, have the storytellers perform their versions for the rest of the group.

POINTS TO REMEMBER

After each teller has developed and rehearsed a story with which he or she feels comfortable, you may want to expand your audience to include other community groups. We found that telling stories in elementary schools, high school and college history and sociology classes, as well as at ours and other senior centers, was an exciting and beneficial experience for all concerned.

It allowed us to gently and comfortably enter the world of theatre and performance while recognizing how valuable our own stories could be to others. Just as the troubadors of yesteryear, we asked for stories from our audience members in exchange for our tellings. Lively tales and discussions grew out of these tellings, and we began to develop a trademark of our future ACTING UP! productions as autobiographical material and audience participation became important parts of our performances.

DEVELOPING CREATIVE WRITING

Many of the storytelling and role-playing activities were developed for creative writing as well as theatrical experiences. Like group improvisations, the guided visualization and imagery tours can lead to writing exercises developed from autobiographical materials. Simply follow the suggested preparation and warm-ups for theatre exercises as they appear in each section, before beginning the related creative writing activities listed below.

INVESTED OBJECT

The Invested Object serves as a memory agent which leads to autobiographical story sources. The Invested Object serves as a launching point for personal recollections, descriptions, imagery and demonstrative writing. One member brought his collection of miniature autos. Estelle spotted the model, double-decker bus, and it brought back the following, delightful memory.

A DEPRESSION ERA MEMORY
by Estelle Jeral

It was in the 1930's. Two good friends and I had been asked for a "date." We were to meet at my house. The three young men were friends whom we had met at school.

We were all gussied up, giggling, excited and waiting for our dates. Around the planned time came our gallant Lochinvars. We chatted and flirted and joked, and then, finally, one of us gals got up the courage to ask where we were being taken. They looked at us and then at each other, as though we had asked the forbidden question.

Would you believe?? They took all the change out of their pockets (no bills) and spread it out on the smoking stand in our living room. Very seriously they counted it two times, so they could determine how far their pooled funds would stretch. After a hurried, whispered consultation, they made the great decision! We were going for a ride to the end of the line on a double-decker bus—which was very popular in those days, particularly on the second level, for rubber-necking in strange neighborhoods—and that wasn't the only necking that was done!

That reminds me of a joke we girls shared between us. About certain fellows we used to say—if they bought you a five cent ice-cream cone, they would try to squeeze it out of you on the way home!

FAVORITE PERSON INTERVIEW

(Stage II - Getting Into Character) Players write dialogue by creating conversations between themselves and their favorite persons. They develop writing skills which include interview-discussion techniques and strong characterizations, as well as playwriting ideas.

One of the ACTING UP! players decided to interview Albert Einstein. The interviewer was a talented tool-and-die maker who had recently been forced into mandatory retirement. He had always admired Einstein, and before the *Favorite Person Interviews,* spent time reading about the life of his hero. He asked Einstein how he felt about being considered a senior citizen in a world that valued productivity above all else. He then asked how Einstein would feel if he were forced into mandatory retirement. The improvisation that grew out of this interview developed into a performance piece called "The Absolutely, Average All-American Senior Citizen." (See Appendix.)

In our performance of this vignette we invited several younger guest artists from a local community college to take roles as members of a glamourous advertising agency which was holding auditions in Senior Centers around the country. They were developing a new ad campaign and were searching for the perfect spokesperson, "The Absolutely Average All-American Senior Citizen." Based on taking a poke at the myth of ageism which claims that all people over sixty-five are alike, this vignette illustrated how unique and productive older people can be throughout their lives. The ACTING UP! player who had first interviewed Einstein now took the role of his hero. Other members of the group became such personal favorites as Helen Hayes, Pablo Casals, Picasso, Benjamin Franklin and other older adults who remained creative in their later years. We also chose examples from our personal acquaintances of people who were active and productive after the age of sixty-five, and added portrayals of them to our vignette. And finally, some of the members of the group chose to play themselves as the vital and growing people they planned to be for the next twenty years. By focusing on the opportunities available to themselves, and those taken advantage of by more famous favorite persons, the players began to crystallize their own philosophies on a successful life over the age of sixty-five.

The advertising interviewers asked questions of their interviewees based upon many of the prejudiced notions our society maintains about elders: "Mr. Einstein, you must be terribly lonely and bored as a senior citizen. You probably sit in the park or play Mah Jong all day." "Ms. Hayes, we all know that successful actresses must be young beauties. What will you do now that you are no longer young?" "Mr. Casals, certainly you are no longer interested in women and love-making at your great age. No senior citizen is interested in sex after sixty-five." "Mr. Picasso, we all know that true creativity is the province of the young. How does it feel to have nothing to do in old age?"

Such a variety of productive accomplishments and activities arose in the interview responses that the flashy advertising agency was forced to abandon its search for "The Absolutely Average, All-American Senior Citizen." They soon discovered that their concept of older people was only a media myth. It was our belief, that by presenting this vignette, our audiences would also abandon some of their prejudices and preconceived notions concerning older adults. After recognizing how rich and productive are the lives of the performers, and the roles they played, it is difficult for an audience to continue to accept the myths that all older people automatically become non-productive, uncreative, and physically and mentally incompetent the moment they reach the age of sixty-five.

SNAP-SHOTS

(Stage II - Living Snapshots) To develop interesting story structure from real-life characters and situations, begin with the given situation in the photograph and develop a written story around it. Writings may focus on the actual situations captured in the photo or be expanded into imaginary incidents and characterizations suggested by the photo.

MY FAIRWEATHER FRIEND
by Paul R. Giardini

He was six feet tall with blond hair, blue eyes and handsome...a lady killer, who swept young ladies off their feet. He was the talk of the community, especially in conversation of females who swooned at the sight of him. He had a suave personality of magnetic quality. Those who knew him called him "Bo."

In the midst of the economic depression of the nineteen- thirties, when most men out of work barely existed from lack of money, Bo drove around the neighborhood in a big, luxurious Packard convertible, in the style of a man of great financial means. One of his trademarks was a beautiful girl seated at his side as he drove around the neighborhood.

I met Bo through a girl I had been dating, who happened to be Bo's cousin. He was a young fellow not much older than I, but had the appearance of an older man. I suppose it was because of the car, the expensive suit and the manner in which he conducted himself...actually, he was twenty-five—two years my senior.

He and I got to be good friends, and on occasions would double-date. He was an individual who always wanted his way as far as dates and entertainment for the evening was concerned. He would arrange all the dates; for me, it was usually a blind date with a girl of his choice, but I never resisted his doing so. The girl was always desirably-beautiful and the envy of others wherever we went.

We would go to dances, night clubs, plays and concerts at Orchestra Hall, but never ever did he permit me to pay part of the cost or tab; he insisted on paying for everything, even the tips to waitresses. He spent money freely and I often wondered where his money came from. It was a treat to be with someone who, in the hard times of an economic disaster, spent money as if it were going out of style. Although I appreciated his benevolence toward me as a friend, I also felt that enough was enough and to go along as a continual free ride was not my nature. I told him that I would like to pay for my own way at least once in a while, that it wasn't fair for him to always pay. He looked down at me with his big blue eyes and said, "Forget it, pal. I enjoy having you with me. I like you and as long as I ask you out with me, it's my show."

My conscience got the best of me when he called me for a Saturday night to go to the movies at his expense, and the girl he had picked for me was the most beautiful ever. I told him that I would not be able to make it. He sounded very hurt by my refusal and said that he was sorry and to let him know if I changed my mind.

Many months passed before I heard from him again; this time he wanted me to go to a dance with him and had picked the girl for me as usual. I agreed and he picked me up with his big car and two gorgeous girls. After the dance, we stopped at a cafe and had a snack or two. The amount of the bill at the cafe was four dollars and fifty cents. I grabbed the check and finally paid the bill. He looked at me, sort of smiled, but didn't say a word. After that, he drove the girls and me home and that was the last time I saw him. I never heard from him again, nor was he seen driving his big car around the neighborhood.

One day, on my way home from work, a newspaper vendor was heard to shout: "Extra, extra, bank robber shot and killed!" I bought a paper and began to read the story which said, "Bosworth Swensen (Bo) was shot and killed late this afternoon while attempting to rob the City Bank." Tears rolled down my cheeks. He had been a good friend, but shouldn't I have suspected him? Maybe so, but I will never forget him.

MAGIC MEMORIES

(Stage II) The acting excercises in Stage II are excellent launching points for oral history gathering and story writing. In one discussion of twentieth century history and its effect on our lives, the players explored landmark periods, e.g., World War I, Depression, the migration West. Memories of Prohibition evoked the following story:

MY MOTHER, THE BOOTLEGGER
by Shirley Helfand

My mother and father were born in Russia, and were married in the town of Minsk. They went to live in Paris, France for about twelve years, with my maternal grandmother. The Yiddish language was not spoken because of so much anti-Semitism there. So the three children, one sister and two brothers, spoke French only.

My family then migrated to the United States in 1917. Father was struggling to make a living. He built his own pushcart, and he and my mother would sell fruits and vegetables, and eke out a living this way.

A short time later they were able to buy a horse and wagon and continue with their peddling. In the meantime I was born and struggled for survival along with the rest of the family.

There were seven of us living in a small, four-room apartment. By the time mother became pregnant with the fifth child, they were able to buy a six-room bungalow. My sister Pearl was born in the new home.

Not long after that, my father got sick and was in and out of hospitals for the next few years. So, in order to be able to feed her family, mother got into bootlegging. This was at the time of Prohibition, so of course her activities were illegal. She did fairly well, until one of the neighbors reported her to the police.

One winter day the kids, plus a couple of their friends, were all at home. There was a knock on the door. A big, Irish plain-clothes-man showed his credentials, came in, and informed my mother that she was violating the law by selling "bathtub gin."

She was expecting this and knew that she was in trouble, so she pretended that she didn't understand. There was a loaf of *challa* bread baking in the oven, and the large tub on the stove was filled with boiling laundry. The baby was crying, and the kids running around in excitement. The steam in the kitchen and the noise from the children was bedlam.

My father was, at this time, in a sanitarium which is now called the "City of Hope." She told this to the policeman and kept saying, "Are you from the hospital? How's my husband?"

For a few minutes the man just stood there and looked around. Then, with a shrug of his shoulders, he pulled out a $5.00 bill, put it on the table and walked out.

DRAMATIC TRAP

(Stage III) Ask writers to write random suggestions on the blackboard or individual slips of paper to fill each of these categories for story structure:

1. Character type: i.e., pregnant sixtyish woman, proud sailor, retired astronaut, talkative pizza delivery person.

2. Location: A place where an unexpected collection of individuals are gathered together. This location sets up the *Dramatic Trap* because it is the agent which pulls together people of unlike minds and backgrounds, forcing them to relate, become acquainted and deepen their understanding of each other; i.e., dentist's office, elevated train or subway, all-night diner, political rally, train station or airport, elevator, movie theatre.

3. Problem/Situation: gives rise to the joint concern that all of the characters will be required to work out together. This problem dictates the situation, but does not dictate the resolution. The writing activity, as in the creative drama improvisation, offers each writer the opportunity to resolve the problem or conflict in a unique and unexpected way, The writers will also be developing the story structure blocks (and theatre improvisation structure) of character development, growth of relationship between characters, posing a conflict or problem to be solved, solution of the problem and resolution of the scene, story and character relationships. Some examples of problem/situations are: The subway train stalls, a hold-up occurs in the dentist's office, a snow-storm forces people to

remain all night at a movie theatre or twenty-four hour diner, people from very different life-styles are supporting the same political candidate at a large rally.

This writing exercise can be an individual experience, or a collaborative story, or playwriting project with groups of four or five people working together. Ask the writers to pick at random one selection from each of the above three categories: *character-type, location,* and *problem/situation.* They will probably want to pick several characters from the *character-type* category. Remind the writers that the most interesting stories and one-act plays grow out of the unexpected. The more unusual the combination of elements in their stories or scripts, the more authentic and true-to-life their writings may be. Whenever the writers seem to get stuck in the development of their work, just remind them to ask the question "What if?" What if the pregnant lady began to have contractions in the stalled train and the only person available to assist her was a Catholic priest? What if young street gang members and a senior citizens' club were stranded all night in a bowling alley because of a blizzard? (For examples of written vignettes, see Appendix, for "The Howard Street EL.")

Concentrate on written pieces and *Guided Imagery Tours* designed specifically to stimulate individual writing activities. Stimulus writings from published collections of oral histories, folktales, historical and period pieces and works of great literature can be most effective when selected by members of the group and read aloud before writing exercises. (See Stage III for further development of *The Dramatic Trap.*)

SELF SYMBOL SEARCH

The self-symbol exercise has its base in the interweaving of contemporary art therapy techniques and the spiritual "journeys" and vision searches of tribal cultures. However, we have used it effectively in elders' groups and intergenerational workshops to stimulate spontaneous writings of deep personal meaning and integrity. We have also introduced these writings as stimuli for candid discussions between age groups (particularly young adults and elders) which offered revealing prejudices and perceptions about self-image and the effects of the aging process. This exercise is the most direct method we have found for converting writing from the expected and the cliche into the authentic and creative. It is also a stimulus which offers seemingly endless possibilities for different types of writing.

You will be leading your group on a series of *Guided Imagery Tours* within which you should allow at least eight to twelve minutes per trip of quiet visualization without interruptions from your voice. The following activity can take place over a period of three or four weeks in which you lead the writers further into their memories and imaginations. You will want to allow these *Guided Imagery Tours* to unfold at a comfortable pace, slowly, and with brief notes (for later reference) taken by the writers after each trip.

After the writers have taken comfortable positions on the floor or in chairs, have them shut their eyes. You may play some carefully chosen recorded music, such as Mozart's "Four Seasons," several of Chopin's Piano Sonatas or chamber music selections from the Baroque period. Or, you may use a small drum, such as bongos, or a large drum, which you beat steadily like a metronome with a wooden mallet at approximately 140 beats per minute (or twice the rate of a human heartbeat). Each leader will also want to develop variations of the *Guided Imagery Tour* to suit her group's particular interest of the moment. The use of an animal or human inner guide for journeying through history, memory or fantasy was the one constant element which we found it helpful to use in all of our journeys.

1. Take the members of the group to a special place in their own childhoods, such as an attic, tree house, closet, hiding place under a bed or the porch, an old trunk or other secret place in which they tucked away treasure and gifts in their childhood. After they have looked carefully around their secret place and have stored away as many specific sensory details as possible, tell them to look around the spot one more time. Tell them that they are to search for an animal guide who will appear to them in a friendly and non-threatening manner. Suggest that this animal does not necessarily have to be real; it may just as well be mythic or an imaginative combination of various creatures.

2. This animal guide will lead them on a journey in which they will walk through some of the rooms and places of their past and present lives. Tell them that they will not have to choose where they will go; the animal guide will make those decisions for them. All they have to do is to follow. Remind them that they will not be afraid as they journey, but will be aware of all their sensory perceptions as they go.

3. After you have led the members of your group to the point where they have journeyed briefly with their animal guides, you will want to explain what self-symbols are. They are objects which exist in our memories, creative fantasies or imaginations which we feel symbolize the most important parts of ourselves. They indicate or encapsulate

our strongest feelings, dreams, desires and attitudes about our lives and the world around us. With the help of their animal guides, ask the writers to begin looking for some or all of the following self-symbols to bring back from their memories and imaginations. Each of the following self-symbol searches may be a separate visualization trip. Ask the players to seek one of the following:

> A geometric shape or uniquely shaped object from nature or life, such as a pyramid, prism, quartz crystal, trumpet, oak leaf, quill pen.

> Two colors which symbolize the duality *and* totality of your unique self.

> A special person from the past. A fantasy character created from the imagination or a character from history or literature similar to the favorite person.

With each of these searches, the travelers must ask their animal guides why these particular self-symbols have been given only to them. Finally, they may ask their animal guides any question of their choice. This will be answered with a "magical object," a gift which will serve them in answering the chosen question as Merlin's wand serves him to answer riddles, puzzles, or to weave "magic spells."

After each of these trips it is wise to have the players write notes of their experiences first and then suggest that they discuss their trips *if they wish*. Often in the act of verbalizing and writing out these rich images, the experiences begin to fall into a much clearer and more meaningful shape.

When the last imagery tour has been taken, ask the players to create individual odysseys or epic poems about their journeys. They will develop a hero/ine who will become their symbolic persona in the epic. They will want to endow this heroic character with all of the virtues, courage and a sense of curiosity and innovation which befits a hero/ine. Others may want to create stories, narratives, songs or poems surrounding individual trips and adventures.

It has been our experience that poetry, fiction and imagery narratives which are drawn from such deep and personal sources as these are wonderful in their lyrical movement, honest self-revelation and unexpected qualities. *Be sure to share your own imagery trip writings with your group.* If you take the time to assist the writers in developing important visualization techniques, the written products of the group's self-symbol search will astonish you with their fresh and poetic vision.

ORAL INTERPRETATION

The creative writings we developed became materials for Readers' Theatre pieces. Each theatre game and improvisation activity can offer your group a wealth of material which deserves to be documented in writing. These pieces deserve to be performed at least once to offer the group a sense of completion of this stage. We have used original materials because they portray our concerns and unique sense of our lives. Another reason for drawing most often from group-developed writings is that so few vital published theatre pieces for elders are available.

One initial performance activity is *Oral Interpretation,* which is the reading aloud of a literary work, choosing pieces that are notable for their expression and imagination. In oral interpretation certain questions come up and should be answered individually by the players:

1. How do I read it to make it dramatic? In each play, story, or poem reading, there is a building action, a climax or high point in the acting just as in a scene. In the reading of the piece, the crisis, climax and resolution should be brought out and emphasized.

2. What specific lines or words in the text should be emphasized either emotionally, or through volume or articulation?

3. What's the level of language used in the work—fancy or colorful—and how do I best convey that language, whether it be colloquial or conversational?

4. What outstanding sensory impressions add to my emotional involvement in the piece. (Refer the players to the sensory exercises in Stage I.)

5. What outstanding sound values can I find in the selection? What words can I make come alive through stressing vowels and consonants, i.e., buzz, swish, boom, heavy, intense; or possible alliteration words, i.e., big bad birds?

6. Can I discover an underlying rhythm to the piece? If it is a poem, can I accentuate the rhythm of the piece?

7. What is the theme or significant message of the work?

Oral Interpretation begins with someone else's work and then progresses to reading our own. The players bring in literature which is their favorite: a poem, a cutting from a play, a short story or a comic essay and read it to the group. They write an introduction which tells the other players how they connect with this work of literature. Tape the players' reading to see how they sound. Retape them, trying experimental changes.

READERS' THEATRE

The difference between Oral Interpretation and Readers' Theatre is a matter of scale. Oral Interpretation is taking one piece of literature or an original work and discovering its richness, spoken before an audience. Reader's Theatre is an ensemble performance for an audience with the script in hand, using eye contact, gestures, facial expression and vocal variety. The responsibility for meaning rests with the interpreter rather than with technical devices of theatre—scenery, lighting, make-up and costumes.

With Readers' Theatre, which is theatre of the mind rather than theatre of the eye, the players can take their own stories and written pieces, cuttings from a play or poems, and put them all together around a central theme: i.e., ageism, the battle of the sexes, love, war, children. To complement their formal storytellings and written works, the players can choose from the slowly-emerging body of dramatic literature dealing with older adults as protagonists, i.e., *On Golden Pond, The Gin Game, Short Plays for the Long Living*. Several selections are contained in this book. You might sponsor a community playwriting contest by and about senior adults, with the prize being the performance of the piece in Readers' Theatre style.

The Reader's Theatre performance can be done by almost any group on a limited or non-existent budget and on any stage space. For the players, Reader's Theatre helps to avoid the problem of self-consciousness and the fear of letting go. With the script in hand, players do not have to be concerned with memorizing lines.

Giving voice to their own works, their own stories and memories, not only reveals the players to the audience, but the players to themselves. They are developing literature which is dynamic, moving, and a highly personal, dramatic creation. Not only does the audience see the human condition through the writers' and performers' eyes, but the oral statements clarify the players' own thinking and give substance, form and validity to their past.

> I used to think of myself as a coloring-book outline. Whatever the world wanted to color me, I reacted to—if they colored me happy, I was; if they colored me boring, I was. But now I see that I have the crayon, and I'm going to color myself all those colors I've never used but always loved!
>
> Bernice

STAGE II - ACT YOUR AGE
EXPLORATION THROUGH IMPROVISATION

"You are old, Father William," the young man said, "and your hair has become very white; and yet you incessantly stand on your head. Do you think, at your age, it is right?"

Lewis Carroll

For my first improvisation Ethel and I were supposed to be in a boat and the boat turned over. I'll never forget my amazement at myself. I "fell" into it as if I had been born into the theatre. There was no embarrassment, no shyness. I found myself swimming on the floor and enjoying it. For the moment it was real; I was there!

Birdell

"Oh, come on! Grow up! Act your age!" How many times have we said words like these, or thought them about an adult who seems to be acting "out of character;" that is, half his age? In our society we feel that the "mature" person must act with decorum; must maintain his dignity. But, this means that the "crazy kid" which we all have lurking within us is supposed to be banished from our behavior. So, an older adult feels guilty when he acts "silly" or tells a joke.

We are afraid of being called "childish," of looking ridiculous in the eyes of our peers. Getting over that stumbling block takes recognition, risk-taking and a lot of laughter. First, we need to recognize that no matter what chronological age we are, we all have a playful, creative, devilish and original kid inside of us who needs to be encouraged to play.

59

The potential for play is within us all. We tend to see playing in terms of the outward spontaneous play of children. Adults play, too; organized games with a winner and loser, like golf, bridge and backgammon. We also play with ideas to solve problems of society. As adults we explore possible alternatives for action by fantasizing different situations and experimenting with our ideas. This imaginative play lends itself to solving problems and creating pathways for bettering society for humankind. However, adults don't often play without a payoff, that is, freely and openly, just to have fun.

Participation in a group such as ACTING UP! is fun. For many older adults, the sense of play which is so important in the development of creative activities is often buried under layers of responsibility, social roles, and rigid expectations fostered by the society in which we live. In a situation where a lifetime work experience, a spouse, a comfortable lifestyle or physical ease of movement have radically changed or disappeared, confidence in oneself is threatened.

This potential for play is the basis of all our work in Stage II. We play our situations so that new possibilities of life can be tried and explored. We are able to open up to new experiences and tap the important creative springs in ourselves only when we feel confident that we will be accepted and appreciated by the group in which we are participating.

> When I was a young girl, I had so much fun. My nickname used to be "Giggles." As I matured and married, I had children and became involved with all the concerns and responsibilities of raising a family. I didn't lose the ability to laugh, but I did misplace that fun-loving "Giggles." Now that I have been with ACTING UP! for five years, I am rediscovering her and I like being me.
>
> Margaret

GUIDELINES

During Stage II of the ACTING UP! process, the members of the group will be learning responsibility for the group as a whole. The players will learn to act as a unit. By setting up certain guidelines to follow, the members of the group can better understand their responsibilities.

1. Use a key word to express that the end of a piece has been completed. By using a word such as "End," "Thank you," or

"Freeze," all the participants, including the audience players, will know that the piece has ended. "Curtain" is a good word for beginning and ending a scene. A scene sometimes can be helped by a word or two of side coaching from the leader.

Sometimes in their enthusiasm, the audience members will respond before hearing the cue word that signals the end of the piece. Remind the players in the audience to wait to respond after they hear a member of the performing group call out the cue word that signals the end of their piece.

2. Be sure the players understand the beginning, middle and end to a piece. Help the players to recognize the elements of conflict and resolution, or more simply, what the problem between the characters is and how they go about solving it.

At the beginning of a story, scene or play, the problem (or conflict) must be explicitly stated. Then the problem has to build through a series of events to a moment in the scene which is the high point of tension (climax). The turning point in the scene is called the crisis. The problem goes one way or the other toward resolution. All improvisations are centered around the idea of two opposing forces in conflict. Conflicts are most often one of the following:

> Human vs. human
> Human vs. self
> Human vs. nature, society or institutions.

3. Encourage listening with interest. Listening with interest is hearing what the other person is saying regardless of what you have to say. You can't really listen well until you quiet all those inner voices. The essence of this encounter is consciously pushing your interests aside and focusing upon what the other person is saying.

4. Recapturing the Highs, or evaluation after every activity, is essential to continue the validation of the group as a whole. What worked and why? Recall things that worked from the dialogue. Recall characterization or interaction between two characters. What made that moment stand out?

Instruct the group to approach every theatre game and improvisation as if it were a mini-performance. This gives dignity to the group. All acting experiences should be approached with great energy and belief in the situation. In other words, they are to play passionately at every game. Each activity has its own sense of value.

Above all, creativity is not limited to one definition. Bill Moyers stated in his television show, *Creativity,* "the most creative people never lose that playfulness, creativeness and zestfulness of youth. Creativity asks first that we remain a perpetual child." When we realize that no one is holding us back, we can open our door to the child within us and begin to play creatively. Playing is important to acting and the theatre because essentially that is the nature of drama: children's games in a more refined form. Elders are experienced players in the game of life.

MUSIC AND MOVEMENT IMAGING

In Stage I the players invested their trust in one another by revealing themselves through personal storytelling. In Stage II the players expand their dramatic vocabulary by becoming physically involved in expressing what they are thinking and feeling as it is happening. This section begins by listening to music and talking about moods and emotions that are evoked by various melodies and styles.

Humans feel the need at times to move to music. A graceful way to bring mental images together with physical interpretation is through movement and expression to music.

This beginning activity starts with an exercise that is familiar to every member of the group. Everyone has some level of experience with music, whether it is listening, humming, singing or dancing. We begin to incorporate body involvement through *Music and Movement Imaging*.

MUSIC

Choose a variety of music (marches, jazz, opera, pop, waltz, rock, classical, folk, country). Ask the players what pictures or images come to mind as they listen to the music. Talk about these images and the moods created by the music. Listen to the music again. This time the players draw images of what the music is expressing to them. Next get the players up and moving freely and spontaneously, each in her own way to the feelings created by the differing moods of the music. Have the players begin to respond by moving their heads, then shoulders, arms, torso, knees and finally, their whole bodies.

Give the players pieces of colored cloth (chiffon scarves) or long pieces of elastic that can be pulled, twisted and stretched. These are additional aids in freeing up the players' body movements.

Choose music representing various ethnic or cultural types, for example, Latin, Slavic, Israeli; Soul or Regge. Players select from the various musical styles to create their own dance steps and teach their dance to the whole group.

Playing a variety of different kinds of rhythm instruments, drums, claves, bells, maracas) or found objects with textural qualities, give each player an opportunity to reclaim the joys of ensemble music. This will be a rhythm band; people of all ages like to create music.

1. Divide the large group into smaller groups of four to five people. Create rhythm patterns in groups. Record the rhythm patterns on a tape recorder.

2. Have the larger group get up and move creatively and spontaneously to the various rhythm patterns.

3. Divide the group into pairs of players. One person in each pair plays the instrument and the other player moves to the feelings and rhythm of the instrument. Then, the instrument player can watch the other player's movement first and create a matching rhythm with her instrument.

4. The leader beats a basic rhythm. One person from the group becomes the leader and teaches the group a "disco dance," making up movements to correspond to the rhythm pattern.

MOVEMENT

Explore a variety of movements, using a tambourine or a drum for background effect. You might try: bouncing like a ball, turning like a top, twisting like a sponge, swinging like a pendulum, hopping like a rabbit, walking with large strides, jumping rope, stretching in the early morning, pushing a heavy rock, pulling a boat on shore, bending to touch toes, shaking loose, trembling like a leaf, whirling in the wind, or squatting while working in the field.

Experiment with everyday movement activities: walk, slide, skip, run, jump, move arms, move legs, change levels, or leap. Have each person select any combination of the above movements and put them into a rhythm pattern, repeating movements, alternating with other movements. Have each player teach his movements to the group.

Explore levels and textures of movement. Try upper, middle and lower levels of these kinds of movement: jerky, sustained, vibratory, swaying, swinging, pulsing.

As for exaggerated movements, explore the following sporting events: swing movements, as in golf, tennis, baseball and bowling; fast movements, as in boxing, hockey and volley ball; slow motion, as applied to moving through water, the Olympics, sportings event on video replay, or walking on the moon where there is little gravity.

PANTOMIME

The players in performance use their bodies as instruments to communicate ideas and feelings. One way to start the development of characterization is to begin with warm-ups involving expression of the body without the voice.

Pantomime is a form of nonverbal communication. The players communicate ideas, moods or activity through action without words, body movement, gesture and facial expression. The players pantomime various activities: e.g., baking a cake, driving a car, painting a house, planting a garden, participating in a sport. Pantomime derives from the first three following exercises:

1. *Isolation exercises:* move one part of the body at a time (hand, shoulder, leg, foot), isolating it from the rest of the body. Alternately, hold one body part still and move around it. Practice creating a pantomime using isolation, i.e., leaning on a window sill, resting a foot on a step.

2. *Tension and release:* practice pantomimes, such as creating a wall, pulling a boat onto shore, pushing a rock, which involve tension and release.

3. *Movement in opposition:* practice pantomimes which involve opposition, such as walking in place, climbing a ladder, tug-of-war.

Other pantomime exercises are:

4. *Object transformation:* Stand in a circle and pass around an imaginary object. Each person shapes or sculpts the space until he creates his own object, showing how to use it. The others should be able to guess what it is.

5. *Everyday tasks:* Each person thinks of a simple task which he does every day. He is to take the task apart and practice pantomiming it, taking each moment to recreate the original sensory feeling.

6. *Charades:* Instead of acting out plays, movies or books, divide into groups of two or three persons and have each group pantomime a three or four-syllable word. Each part of the word requires a separate scene acted out to illustrate the syllable and whole word.

7. *Silent movies:* Take suggestions from the group for scenes which can be entirely acted out in pantomime, scenes which lend themselves to non-verbal action. Show how much is communicated without words.

8. *Mirror imagery:* Divide the group into pairs, each one facing her partner and staring directly into the pupils of her eyes. One person is the mirror reflection and the other is the person looking into the mirror. The initiator of the action moves very slowly as the mirror image follows exactly what she is doing (movements and facial expression). Maintain concentration so that the pair is working as one unit.

9. *Sporting events:* Any kind of sporting activity is good for pantomime and can be a good warm-up or energizer; for example, tug-of-war (two teams), baseball game, bowling. Play with an imaginary ball, tossing it from one player to another and changing the size and weight of it as it goes around the room.

10. *Silent conflict:* This is good for stressing meaning on the non-verbal level. Two people have a conflict which cannot be spoken. The audience guesses what is happening between the two people. Do the scene over, adding dialogue, but try to retain all the sub-text and non-verbal communication.

11. *Demonstrating emotions:* Some good emotions for pantomime are admiration, affection, anxiety, anger, boredom, cheerfulness,

despair, impatience, sadness, surprise, satisfaction. Demonstrate emotions, using in order: voice only, face only, whole body; then the body and voice.

PANTOMIME WALKS

There are several different kinds of walks that can be used for *Music and Movement Imaging*. One such walk is the Rhythm Walk, which is rhythm as it pertains to character. Each character in a play or scene has a movement quality or rhythm quality which makes him unique. Illustrate different kinds of characters through movement and rhythm; for example, staccato or languid movements.

In Orff exercises, the walk involves a short chant along with body movement. One such Orff exercise is "Shake Those Simmons Down," in which the players stand in a circle. The whole group first circles to the right, then to the left. Each person takes a turn leading the group in any kind of body movement. Encourage the group to be as imaginative and free as possible. One person moves and the whole group imitates her, ending with touching the toes. The chant is:

> Do like this, do, oh, do, oh.
> Do like this, do, oh, do, oh.
> Do like this, do, oh, do, oh.
> Shake those simmons down.

In "Strut, Miss Mary," the group divides into two lines facing one another, so that each person has a partner. Beginning with one line, the first person walks down the middle aisle as silly as he is willing to do and his partner follows, imitating exactly the walk he observed. Each one has a turn to lead off and have a partner follow. As the players walk, they rhythmically chant:

> "Strut, Miss Mary, strut Miss Mary, strut Miss Mary
> all day long.
> Here comes another one, just like the other one,
> Here comes another one all day long."

In *Occupation Walk*, the players walk around the room in a circle. The leader calls out different kinds of characters and the players move as if they are that character. The leader calls out "Freeze" and approaches one player with a question to which he must respond in character. Some examples for characterizations are: lifeguard, waiter, ballet dancer, caveman, disco dancer, Miss Universe, Mr. America, juggler, spy, queen/king, clown.

OTHER FORMS OF NON-VERBAL COMMUNICATION

Speaking in "gibberish" (made-up sounds that have no word meanings) is helpful in developing expressive, larger-than-life body movements and vocal inflections. Each player sells a product using gibberish. The other players, observing, should be able to identify the product by the player's body movements, facial expressions and vocal inflections.

For *Tribal Gibberish* separate the players into two groups, each group representing a tribe living in an arid land. The leader assigns a subject on which the players are to talk in gibberish. One example could be that the players are going on a journey to hunt for more water/food/better shelter. A decision must be made to get the neighboring tribes' water supply. Other rituals than can be acted out which are universal to every culture are: birth, death, marriage, the hunt, war and the ceremony celebrating the transition from childhood to adulthood. Within their tribe the players begin by inventing a group chant, for example, "jay jay co lay,jay go veeca, go veeca longa, longa too monga, hey a yay day." The observing tribe must be able to tell what the other tribe is talking about through the acting tribe's body movements, facial expressions and vocal inflections.

All these movement and imaging exercises are ways to motivate the players to begin using their bodies as instruments for communicating ideas and feelings. The following two activities, the *Emotional Sculpture* and *The Machine*, are especially helpful in getting the group up on its feet to make this new stage of expression work.

EMOTIONAL SCULPTURE

Emotions are the wellspring of our energy to get up and become involved. In the *Emotional Sculpture,* the players combine their energies to create a statue of one emotion.

WARM-UPS

Contort your facial muscles into different emotions. Use music or clap a rhythm pattern to change facial expressions.

Pick one emotion and talk about it.

Use lead lines such as, "I am happy because ....," "I am most happy when ....," "Happiness (or any other emotion) is ...." Sit or stand in a circle, so that each player completes the phrase. Try several different emotions.

Remain in the circle and add a physical expression to each phrase. If someone says, "I'm happy because someone loves me," she might hug herself tightly. One of the ACTING UP! players said, "I am happy because I can play golf all day on Wednesdays." He made the motion of swinging a golf club.

Other emotional-recall lead lines are : "I love," "I hate," "I get angry when...." When a player is telling a story surrounding one of these feelings, ask him to allow the group to see the total memory; how he felt inside; his gut reaction to the experience.

THE ACTIVITY

Divide the players into two groups. One group performs; the other becomes the audience and observes. The first player moves as quickly as possible from one side of the room to the other, speaking the emotion she chooses as loudly as possible. Energy adds momentum and life to the piece. After she calls out the emotion, she freezes (stops short and remains motionless) in a position that displays the meaning she sees in that emotion. After the first person is in place (depicting "happiness," for instance), the next player in line comes forward energetically, repeats the word ("happy"), and adds her physical attitude about happiness to the already-frozen picture. Continue until each player becomes a part of a "statue of happiness."

POINTS TO REMEMBER

In *Emotional Sculptures,* each player should be touching another, so that some part of each person's body is in physical contact with the whole.

There are many levels at which each player can work, for example, standing, sitting, crouching or reaching. The entire stage is at his disposal.

Players quickly learn to assume positions which they can hold for extended periods while the audience observes. A few players will adopt strenuous poses from time to time. They should be reminded to take positions they can hold comfortably for several minutes.

Remind players to use facial expressions to show emotion.

While the players hold a position representing an emotion, the audience may walk among the players, as if observing a statue in a public park. This will add a new dimension as the audience interacts with players in the scene.

VARIATIONS

1. After the players are in position and holding one emotion, ask the audience to suggest another emotion. The players think and move for a few seconds, changing their physical position into a picture of the new emotion, remembering to touch one another at some point. If movement continues, the leader may call out "Freeze," and the players halt, while the audience observes and then suggests another emotion. As the group continues through several differing emotions, both players and audience will gain understanding of the skill involved in forming a "stage picture"—a pleasing and interesting presentation of form and space on stage.

2. The players show an emotion only through facial muscles. To begin, call out an emotion, which the players portray through facial expression. They then proceed to expand the emotion through exaggerated facial contortion. think of the face as a Greek mask and show one emotion as vividly as possible with eyes, nose, cheeks and mouth. Each player's face seems to explode with emotion.

The choice of emotions to try is vast. Some selections are: admiration, affection, anxiety, anger, boredom, cheer, despair, impatience, sadness, surprise, satisfaction, happiness, jealousy, joy, nervousness, relief, despondency, infatuation, fright, reverence, shock, power, embarrassment, pride, relaxation, loneliness and zest.

3. Combine facial and full-body expressions of emotion. The leader may direct the players to thrust their bodies through space and then freeze into position, holding a physical and facial pose of the emotion simultaneously. Repeat the previous body movement, this time vocalizing the emotion—making sounds which express the emotion without words. Now, repeat the body movement, this time adding words, each player speaking to himself. For example, in one instance the emotion was fear. The players responded with such lines as, "Oh, no, please don't hurt me," "Oh, I just can't go out in front of all these people." Repeat again, this time adding dialogue, so that two players verbalize the emotion to each other. This will expand to a full-group scene with all members involved in the same emotion and expressing it to one another.

Ask the players what was the most interesting, thought-provoking or exciting "emotion" experience they had.

THE MACHINE

Creations which are group-oriented enhance the players' ability to work together. No one feels singled out or put on the spot to perform. Ultimately these activities develop a group cohesiveness and ensemble spirit, so vital to Stage III: the performance stage.

WARM-UPS

Form a circle. The leader initiates specific movements that everyone imitates, for example, clapping hands or bending from side to side. When the leader calls, "Change," the person to his left begins a new movement which the group duplicates. As members in turn continue to initiate movements, players begin to move to different rhythms.

The second time around the circle, use sounds which each player imitates. The players may use their names or non-verbal sounds. To vary the sounds, whisper them or repeat them loudly. Slow them down or speed them up. Talk about different kinds of machines, their working parts and the sounds they make. Machine examples are: toaster, coffee pot, steam shovel, blender, washing machine, dryer, drill, saw, train, helicopter, alarm clock, vacuum cleaner.

THE ACTIVITY

In the following activity it is not necessary to make a specific machine. It is more important to have the group up and moving rhythmically together as parts in a spontaneous machine. Before beginning, remind the players that when one part of the machine is not working, the whole machine malfunctions. One player begins a repetitive motion—a continuous motion and sound, such as swishing, sighing, whistling—in center stage. One by one the players add onto the first player's motion by filling the void with an action complementary to the first player. Once everybody is involved in the machine, the activity may end by turning off the switch. Or, the machine may break down, run out of fuel, or go so fast that it blows up like scattered debris.

The leader may control certain activities of the machine with instructions to the members to change the rate, volume or pitch of their sounds and movements.

Review the *Points To Remember* listed after the *Emotional Sculpture,* in regard to touching, levels of play, facial expression and avoiding strain.

VARIATIONS

When the players have mastered the simple machine with moving parts and sounds, they may divide into smaller groups of four to five members to create their own machine subsequently presenting it to the group. The machine may be ordinary or fanciful, i.e., a lawn mower, typewriter, popcorn machine, or computer; wild and mythical, such as a silly-putty assembly machine, anti-gravity machine, shrinking machine, or a bubble machine.

RECAPTURING THE HIGHS

Take the time to get the players' feedback. What were their best moments, their most successful machines, and why? What were some of the notable facial expressions, sounds and movements? What were some of the innovative ways used by the players to become a part of *The Machine?*

THE TELEPHONE CONVERSATION

Using the telephone as a prop assists players to assume character roles and aids them in making their actions on stage believable. Since it is something to hold onto, the phone acts as a physical support. The telephone can sometimes "outwit" a player's fear or stage fright because we tend to associate talking on the phone with being heard, rather than being seen on stage.

WARM-UPS

One player tells a short story about something that happened in the past day or two. Then, another player repeats as many details of the same story as she can remember, imitating the person's physical and vocal gestures and mannerisms. Women and men may discover interesting perceptions while exchanging gender roles in this way.

One person whispers a phrase or statement to the person nearest him and the thought gets passed around the room with the last person to receive the phrase saying it aloud. This is similar to the familiar children's game of "gossip," an exercise in listening and focusing precisely on the speaker's words.

Add-a-Word Story is done with the group seated or standing in a circle. The first person begins a story with four words, for example: "On one dark night...." The next person adds another four words to the emerging sentence, and so on, until a story is formed. It is not necessary for each player to repeat the previous words, only to add new ones to make up the story. In a variation of this warm-up, the leader lets each player tell the story until the instruction, "Switch," moves the story to the next teller, who must pick up the story and continue from the moment the previous player stopped.

What Are You Taking? is a memory-stretching warm-up. The first player says, "I'm going on a vacation and am going to take my toothbrush." The next player repeats the last item and adds a new one. Each player repeats the whole list, until only one player can remember the complete list.

Note: This is a good place to repeat the *Duo Storytelling* activity outlined in State I. Instead of using written autobiographical stories, the players continue to improvise and develop spontaneous stories.

THE ACTIVITY

The players discuss possible situations that might come up in a phone conversation that would be good for improvisation. Think of topical and timely issues that would be of interest to the group.

Two players carry on a telephone conversation solving one problem between the two of them. Provide the group with a sample list of possible characters to choose from: barber, hairdresser, teacher, plumber, policeman, baker, telephone operator, clergyman, doctor, psychiatrist, exterminator, spouse, child, mayor, telephone surveyor, historical or popular figures of the day. Once two players have decided on who they are going to be, they must come up with a mutual problem to solve during their telephone conversation.

POINTS TO REMEMBER

Set the stage with two chairs, situated so that the players are not facing each other; although they may be able to see one another. Encourage the players to include the audience in their conversation by speaking loudly enough to be heard.

VARIATIONS

1. Carry on a telephone conversation in which both parties have conflicting problems to solve. For example, a salesperson wants to interest a housewife in aluminum siding for the house; the housewife wants to prepare supper for her husband, his boss and the six chidren; or, a retired homeowner talks to her senator about social security cutbacks.

2. Carry on a telephone conversation on a party line with four people trying to hold two conversations about two problems.

3. Carry on a lines-crossed conversation with four people holding two conversations, but with four problems or conflicts going on. These variations help players learn to give and take. Give and take is a rapport between the players and a developing sense of when it is appropriate to speak or move and when it might be better to stop or remain silent.

The players are also learning to switch the "focus" from one area of the stage to another. Focus is the technique of drawing the audience's attention to a particular action taking place on stage. Ways to take focus would be to stand in front of someone, to talk louder than everyone else, to go downstage center, to be on a higher level than anyone else, to be wearing some costume that is bright or out of the ordinary. Even making faces or exaggerated body movements can capture the focus. As the players experiment with these complicated focus situations, allowing the scene to go where it may, they get better at working cooperatively as actors to make the scene interesting and, at the same time, clear to the audience.

RECAPTURING THE HIGHS

Talk about what worked and why. Define together the conflicts and resolutions of each conversation. Did the prop telephone help to keep the players' concentration on the scene and on their individual character roles? Were the players able to share or exchange the focus?

ACTING UP! developed one of its scripts for performance from this telephone improvisation. It is entitled *Point-Counterpoint* and can be found in the Appendix.

ROLE-PLAYING AND IMPROVISATION

> We started improvising scenes. It was then that I told
> one of the women that I was finished. I stayed away
> maybe one week. Well, with a little bit of persuasion
> and a lot of warmth and understanding from a group
> of people, I came back. So from a "shy violet" I became
> a "rambling rose." I lost a lot of inhibitions and
> learned to like me.
>
> Sarah Lee

The *Telephone Conversation* is the beginning of role-playing, taking on and playing a character other than oneself. Role-playing enables players to understand themselves from different viewpoints, and broaden their picture of themselves in relation to the world. The players try on parts which they haven't played in life. They will discover the roots for many different roles in themselves as they emphasize various aspects of their own characters in role-playing.

ACTING UP! relies on improvisation for character development because it unconsciously draws on many of the resources each player brings to the group, because there is no memorization involved to inhibit or artificially direct the players, and because there is no "right" or "wrong" interpretation of a character. An "anything goes" attitude prevails within the ACTING UP! troupe and encourages risk-taking. Within the safety of the supportive group the players are encouraged to investigate the varied facets and emotional levels inherent in their personalities.

All theatre is autobiographical, even if it is fantasy. Saul Bellows once said, "If the character we are creating seems flat, we must be charitable and give of ourselves." Relying on our life experiences, each human carries the seeds of all characters.

> For the first time in my life, I'm stepping out of my own
> role, the role the world sees me in, and I'm projecting
> thoughts I've always wanted to share.
>
> Maury

A player must first create his role to know who his character is. Improvising begins with the actions he takes in that role. Asking the following questions is the necessary groundwork before beginning an improvisational scene.

WHO, WHERE, WHEN, WHAT AND WHY

WHO?: Who are you? What kind of character are you? Are you old or young? How do you move? What's your voice like?

WHERE?: Where does the scene take place? What is the environment like? Is it familiar or is it strange? Is it hot or is it cold? Is it open or crowded? Are you inside or outside?

WHEN?: When is the story/scene taking place? What historical period: past, present or future? What is the time of day?

WHAT?: What is the conflict or problem to be solved? What are you as the character going to do about it?

WHY?: How is the character feeling and why?

CONFLICT GAME

The players are not only learning to emphasize new parts of themselves, but also to react to other players' characters. Their work becomes a communion, without which, Stanislavski maintains, there is no real acting. The players learn that improvising requires continuous interaction with the other players. Role-playing and exchanging roles with other players allows not only peers, but people of all ages, to try on the *persona* of another person. Tolerance grows; prejudice falls away, resulting in natural human compassion, understanding, and a willingness to set things right.

In the *Conflict Game* we combine the elements of a good story (Who, Where, What, When and Why) with conflict and resolution, the elements of a good dramatic plot. More simply put, conflict resulting in resolution equals dramatic plot. Michael Shurtleff, in his book, *Audition,* lists the juxtaposition of opposites as one important guidepost to acting: "Consistency is the heart of dull acting...all dramatic relationships are competitive."

In one improvisation using two hats, Bernice selected a floppy rain hat and Joe selected a Tom Sawyer-type hat. These hats suggested a fishing scene to the players, who became a husband who loves "goin' fishin'" and a wife who hates the sport. They sat together in the rain at his favorite spot trying to have fun. The improvisation developed into a couple who have been going through this routine for years, ending with the lines:

She: "How did I ever get into this situation?"
He: "I don't know about you, but I know what happened to me. I married you!"

Bernice remarked that she was able to get angry and really let her stage husband have it! This was something she was not able to do in her own life. When Joe asked her to clean and cook the fish, she remarked, "You caught it, so you can clean it, and cook it and I hope you choke on it!" This was not only a scene with conflict but became a wonderful release of anger for Bernice in a safe situation. Joe had a great time playing off her anger.

WARM-UPS

Opposites is a warm-up in which the players divide into two lines facing each other. The players in one line know a specific action which they will pantomime. The players in the other line must guess the action and perform its opposite. For example, if the first line players are performing an action of happiness, the other line players would pantomime sadness. Other possibilities include love/hate, push/pull, stare/look away, lift/lower, throw/catch, sink/swim, hot/cold.

In *Friends and Enemies,* partners are chosen and action is improvised as if the partners were best friends and then as if they were worst enemies. The activity can be done in pantomime first and then dialogue added. Notice the differences in voice and body movements which show the contrasts between the "friends" situation and the "enemies" situation. Activities to pantomime include: eating dinner while seated side-by-side; dancing together at a dance class; playing golf as partners in a tournament; painting a room with someone; entering a bus together that has only one empty seat.

In *Take a Stand,* one group of players takes a stand on an issue; a second group opposes the viewpoint of the first group. Each group voices its views; then viewpoints are switched and argued from the opposite position. It helps to give one player the role of interviewer, as if for a television show. After the exercise, the players discuss feelings which emerged during the exercise.

THE ACTIVITY

Members are asked to play people with definite conflicting needs and desires. The players begin by fleshing out their characters—Who they are; What they're doing; Where the scene takes place; When it occurs; and Why it is happening. The unknown condition is the outcome of the story. When the resolution is unknown it increases the involvement of the players with their individual characters. Uncertainty heightens the players' energy, when each character is trying to fulfill his desires and goals. Without a script defining the winners and losers, each player tries hard to succeed. This is the action of much daily life drama. Some conflict situations that have worked well for us are:

A policeman stops a speeding driver for running a stop light. The policeman wants to give a ticket or his chief will give him demerits; the driver wants to be let off the hook or his license will be revoked and his wife angry.

A grocer and a customer come into conflict when the customer brings back a partially-used, faulty product, and the grocer refuses to return the money because the product has been used.

One player wants to date another, but the second plays hard-to-get on the assumption that it will attract the other's interest.

A husband wants to use the family money to buy a new car; the wife wants a family vacation.

A parent asks a grandparent to babysit; the grandparent would rather join the daughter at the movies or shopping.

An elderly parent wants her children to visit. The offspring feel pressured for time and resist.

Players choose issues that are pertinent to their lives. The players switch roles, thereby playing both roles and experiencing both sides of each issue.

VARIATIONS

1. Divide into small groups of three or four. Give each group the same starting instructions of character and situation. When the groups work separately, they will develop unique conflicts and resolutions. Each group runs through its improvisation several times and then presents it to the entire group. Each sub-group will show a different beginning, middle and end to its improvisation. This variation illustrates that improvisation does not involve "right answers," but creative thinking by each individual.

2. Try the first variation again, but this time the scene begins and ends with the same line of dialogue. Give the players one line that is to be said as the first and last line of the scene.

3. Each player chooses an animal role. He struts, prances or slithers across the stage. The players then evolve their animal characters into a human role. With the help of the leader, the players pair up for an improvisational scene. For example, through their interaction, a "roosterlike" man and an "Angora catlike" woman inform the audience of their relationship.

RECAPTURING THE HIGHS

Talk over the feelings of being on opposite sides of a conflict. How did it feel to switch roles with your antagonist? When talking over the conflicts and resolutions, discuss other alternative activities which may have been possible within your character.

LIVING SNAPSHOTS

In *Living Snapshots* the elements of a good story are assembled in order to create the book's first improvisational scene. Utilize the personal photograph as a starting point from which to reach out for improvisation materials. Concentrate on the moment of the photograph and the immediate relationships, individual emotions and story-line.

The act of recapturing personal scenes for dramatic interpretation helps to build the actor-writer's confidence in the validity and importance of his life experiences and the value of communicating these experiences to others. There is a dramatic honesty implicit in the moment captured in a photograph which can transform an improvisation into a poignant or funny scene. These activities are meant to stimulate the actors' interest in dramatic moments caught in a photo—to go on knowing the characters captured there, to begin the "what if" process which leads to longer scenes and playwriting.

Bernice, a shy and witty ACTING UP! player had been interested in playwriting for sometime, but had not gathered the confidence to begin. She spoke often about how difficult it was to find a moment from her life which she felt was meaningful enough to develop into a completed vignette. The day we asked the ACTING UP! members to bring photos for *Living Snapshots,* Bernice took a risk and brought a snapshot from a humorous, but embarrassing, incident that occurred when she was in high school.

She and her fellow students were on a botany field-trip with their prim and near-sighted botany teacher. Bernice had worn her expensive new jodphurs because she knew that a certain young man would also be on the field trip. However, the entire class had to cross a shaky log which spanned a swiftly moving stream. And as Bernice said, "I get dizzy whenever I see a glass of water coming toward me. You can imagine how terrified I was to walk across that log!"

In the improvised dramatization of the story behind the snapshot, the players created a believable and exciting chain spanning the tipsy log, helping each other across, Bernice was left on the other side, fearing that she would fall in the water and ruin her new pants. So all the boys were asked to turn their heads while she crossed the log in her red flannel bloomers. But of course, that certain special boy had brought along his Brownie camera. And in the midst of her terrified crossing, Bernice was captured, on film, in her underwear. Bernice's last line of dialogue was, "That brat, Tom, caught me in my bloomers for all posterity. And if that wasn't enough, he made wallet-sized photos of this scene for everyone in the class to remember me by!"

79

After experiencing the excitement of not only acting, directing and narrating, but also of seeing her own story come to life through the humorous improvising of her fellow players, Bernice made this comment:

> I don't think I ever would have gotten the nerve to tell that story, let alone act in it, if it hadn't been for the safety of the group. The people in the group made me feel supported. After I saw how really interesting my story was when we acted it out, I realized I had broken through all sorts of inhibitions and barriers, and I had come out a gutsy comedienne!

WARM-UPS

Bring personal photos to the workshop which you feel will stimulate conversation and are active, humorous and evocative. If possible, bring old photographs from your family's past, as well as more recent snapshots. Ask the actors to bring photos which have a story connected with them; for example, grandparents posing on their arrival in America; winning a tango contest with an old boyfriend; sporting events; Christmas in the year that everyone had the flu; the family at the state fair; parents posing with their first child; "working" photographs, such as coal mining, farming, office photos.

Try to include a variety of locations, events, historical periods, plus representative ages through the actors' lives. Also ask the actors to bring photos which have at least two characters in them, if possible.

Pass the photographs around, or project them onto a screen or wall using an overhead projector. Ask the person whose photo is being discussed not to give any information about the photo. This allows the other players to develop ideas around the photos which have a meaning for the entire group. Discuss the following questions:

What do you see in the "physical picture" of the photo?

Without being acquainted with the people, what do you know of their relationships with each other by the way they interact physically?

Who is looking at the camera? Who is looking away? Why?

Is someone caught in the act of speaking? What is he saying?

Who is the photographer? What is that person saying to the group?

What feelings are shown in the groups' facial expressions and physical gestures?

What do you think happened just before the photo was taken? Just after?

What is the person in the photo thinking about? the photographer?

What is the scene or event that stimulated this photo?

What kind of emotional response does the photo elicit from you?

THE ACTIVITY

In *Living Snapshots,* we work solely with autobiographical materials drawn from the players' memories, family folklore and cultural mythology. These are then transformed through improvisations into short dramatic sketches in which the author of the story may choose to play herself. The scene is being acted out spontaneously as the story is being told by the narrator-actor.

The person to whom the photo belongs becomes the narrator-director of the scene. She chooses the actors for each role and positions them in a tableau which duplicates the photograph. (One of the most important characters is the photographer, because it is he who cues the end of the scene.) While the actors are in position on stage, have the narrator-director describe her characters to the players. How old are they? What is the relationship between them? How do they feel about having the photo taken? The actors should ask questions about their characters until everyone is comfortable with his or her role. The narrator-director should be the only person making comments to the actors. The rest of the players make up the audience for the improvisation and should be paying attention in preparation for their performances.

The actors take their places to one side of the stage while the narrator-director begins to tell the story which surrounds the shooting of the photograph. (The narrator-director may choose to play herself in the scene or may choose someone else to take her place.)

The improvisation ends with a tableau or "physical picture" approximating the actual photograph. Be sure to make it clear to the players that the *Living Snapshot* scenes in these activities end with the moment that the photograph is taken.

POINTS TO REMEMBER

It might be a good idea for you, as leader, to be ready to use one of your own photographs.

Are the players clear about the story line? (Who, What, Where, When and Why). Who are they? Where are they? What is happening and Why? The players must relate to each other as they move to create the photo. All players should be aware of each other through gesture, expression and touch. The players should understand that they are part of the same photo.

VARIATIONS

1. Break up into smaller groups of four or five and ask each group to select a photograph and a narrator-director. Have each group spend no more than ten minutes listening to the character descriptions and the story behind the photograph from the narrator-director. Under the guidance of the narrator-director, each group will develop an improvised scene. This scene will end in a still tableau as the photographer freezes the action of the story.

2. *Caught-in-the Act* involves three to five players who take their places on stage. The leader suggests a situation, a location or an activity in which the actors are to perform. For example, you are a crack surgical team, preparing to perform open heart surgery to save a life (nurses, anesthesiologists, surgeons, patients). In another situation, you just won a game against your biggest rival (cheerleaders, football players and friends). You are celebrating this big victory to the hilt. The players move randomly on stage, becoming the character they wish to be, at the same time, observing the other players and their character relationship to one another. When they seem to be in character, the leader calls, "Freeze photo," and the players form a picture on stage as if they had just posed in-character for a photograph.

3. *Historical Caught-in-the Act* uses the same guidelines as above, except the situation calls for situations and characters from history. For example, you are the Wright brothers and friends at Kitty Hawk and the wind is right for launching your airship— "Freeze photo." Or, you are at the Bastille and the gates are locked, but you have lots of friends with the same idea, "Down with the monarchy!"— "Freeze photo!"

RECAPTURING THE HIGHS

Once a story is being acted on stage, it belongs as much to the players as it does to the person who told the story.

There is no "right" or "wrong" in the players' individual interpretations. If the story-line differs through improvisation from the original telling, this adds new dramatic levels to the actual story. Emphasize these points throughout all improvisations drawn from autobiographical material.

The flow of the scene and the spontaneous discoveries and exchanges between the players always take precedence over the "facts" of the original idea. This allows room for experimentation, risk-taking and character-development experiences. The narrator-director has brought the raw materials for a dramatic idea. Feelings such as "but that wasn't how it really happened—it happened this way" are secondary to transforming the original idea into an exciting, workable improvisation.

MAGIC MEMORIES

Telling a story on stage—including the conflict, climax, resolution, and elements of character—makes a dramatic piece possible. In *Magic Memories*, we explore the possibilities for good improvisational material by using the players' memorable stories from the past as the basis of the exercise. The players act out the memories from the past, creating new stories, embellishing the details, and gaining from the spontaneity and interaction of the other players.

WARM-UPS

As a warm-up for *Magic Memories*, we repeat a previous warm-up called *Lead Lines* (See the *Emotional Sculpture*). Sitting in a circle, each player completes the phrase, "I love...," "I hate....," "I was so thrilled when....," "I got angry when....," "I'm happy because....," "I hope....," "I was scared when....," or "I cried when....."

Ask specific questions regarding players' past lives, especially dramatic firsts, for example:

What was the first car you rode in?

When was the first time you drove?

What was the first movie you saw?

What was your first trip away from home?

Who was your first good friend?

What was your first paying job?

What was your first deep disappointment?

What was memorable about your first kiss?

What is your first memory of school?

Talk about how things were done differently in your early life, compared to these days. For instance, how did you wear your hair? What dances were popular when you were a teenager? What styles of clothes were popular in your teens? What kind of pranks were pulled in the classroom? How was transportation different then and now? What do you remember getting into trouble for?

Another wellspring of ideas is in history. History records high and low points of existence: depressions, wars, marriages, discoveries, great sporting accomplishments, riots, births and deaths, all of which provide a wealth of material for human drama.

For other materials, refer to the written autobiographical pieces and oral history storytelling developed in Stage I, Storytelling: History Is Our Story.

THE ACTIVITY

Telling stories is an excellent vehicle for improvisational play. *Magic Memories* uses living memories as story-telling stimulus. After the players have related memories from the past (sharing their outstanding moments of childhood, home, school, first jobs, romances), several stories are chosen to relive through improvisation. The leader chooses players for the parts in the story. The storyteller may play herself or someone else, or may choose to sit back and watch her story come to life. Remind the storyteller to allow for individual variations as other players recreate the situation on stage. There are three simple variations to this basic activity. The first involves total narration. As the storyteller tells her story the players pantomime the action as the story is being told. The second variation is the storyteller participant. The storyteller not only tells the story, but as the action is going on, she also plays herself. The third way begins with the storyteller telling her story and at some point (which can be designated by a verbal cue from the leader), she hands the conclusion of the story over to the other players...as if she is saying, "Now it belongs to you." The other players may then:

1. Change the ending of the story.
2. Add another conflict or a different one.
3. Change the character elements.

VARIATIONS

1. *Add to the Action "A"* has one person beginning an activity in pantomime. Activities such as planting a garden, cooking, picnicking or going to the beach are good for pantomime. As other players identify what is going on, they join the action, each doing a different activity that relates to the scene created by the first player. After five or six people have entered the scene, the leader calls, "Freeze," and the actors hold their positions. The leader then calls, "Add dia-

logue," and the players continue the scene, talking to each other in character. As the players become aware of an audience watching them, they begin taking turns speaking and listening, so that only one speaks at a time. This allows the focus to change from one player to another and the scene to grow from climax to resolution.

2. *Add to the Action "B"* continues performing the previous activity. The leader calls out, "Freeze," and the players stop the action. On the cue, "Slow motion," they continue in pantomime, but slowly, as if moving though molasses. Then the leader calls out, "Fast motion," and the players proceed to pantomime rapidly. Finally, the leader calls out "Freeze...add dialogue and end the scene." The players quickly resolve the conflict(s) and bring the activity to a successful end.

3. The audience participates in *Interviewing the Man on the Street.* Choose a location in which many people of different backgrounds would be together, for example, the airport. One player is the interviewer working for a television news team. Let the audience suggest a topic for the interview. The players on stage agree to pass or play. If they pass on a suggestion, they would like another subject from the audience. When they agree to play, the action begins. Each player on stage has chosen a character to play in this location, for example, a foreign woman, a nun, a stewardess, businessman, airplane pilot, nuclear war protestor. The interviewer chooses one of the players milling about or working in the situation. When she starts the interview, everyone else freezes until the interview is finished and she begins to look for someone else to interview.

4. The players developed their own variation which they entitled *Fantasies and Dreams.* The players share their fantasies and dreams, first with one other member of the company in pairs and then with the entire group. Choose a fantasy or dream and make it come true. The desire to have it become reality is motivation for acting it out, not only for the player who has the dream, but also for the other players in their desire to have the dream come true for their fellow player.

Mary K. took the part of a young girl whose doll had broken. She screamed and cried until someone came to comfort her. She remarked that as a child she never could display her feelings overtly and that doing so on stage felt very good. She said, "When I play the little girl—I'm not me any more at all. For that moment I am the little girl I would have liked to have been."

One day Bernice, a soft-spoken gentle lady with a child-like sense of fun, revealed in our discussion of *Fantasies and Dreams* that for one day in her life her secret wish was to be the most scintillating character in the room, a true "life of the party!" The players got together between rehearsals and planned a surprise improvisation which would allow Bernice to have her wish. Everyone except Bernice came early to the next rehearsal. When Bernice arrived, the improvisation began and she was feted, cheered and celebrated at the "Bernice Appreciation Ceremony." Each of the players "toasted" her, declaring what he or she appreciated most about Bernice. The vignette ended as Bernice was ceremoniously lowered into the imaginary punch bowl.

There is a strong need and great potential, among older adults, to complete what is called "unfinished business." These are the fantasies and dreams which we had as a child, teen or young adult, but were never able to make "happen" because the circumstances or needs of the moment made their strong demands. By acting out these: "I should have," "I wish I had," "what if," "how about it," "I always dreamed," "I used to fantasize that," we don't actually make them come true, but we create the possibility that they can be made to happen on stage as if it were a reality. On an emotional level, it achieves the required *catharsis;* that is, a letting go, a release of stored-up emotion which can be ventilated in order to reach a state of equilibrium. In this way the players are able not only to share their fantasies and dreams, but give them a sense of completion or closure.

THE TABLEAUX

A specific activity for developing spontaneity and improvisation is *The Tableaux*. The players are asked to perform on the spot without forethought or special preparation. Through this activity the members of the troupe see the benefits of an interesting visual composition, that is, the picture the audience sees on stage. In *The Tableaux*, the players come into physical contact in quick-thinking situations. In turn, these exercises help the growth of spontaneous and intuitive reactions among the members.

WARM-UPS

In *Who Started the Action*, one person is sent out of the room, while the others stand in a circle. Decide who will start the action which everyone in the circle will follow. The outside player comes back into the middle of the circle and watches everyone carefully to see if he can guess who the leader is. The leader must change the action frequently so that the person in the middle may have a chance to guess. This exercise involves careful observation and concentration.

In *Last One In,* one player leaves the room while three or four players begin an improvised scene knowing the circumstances (Who, What, Where, When and Why). The outside player enters the room and must fit into the scene by watching, listening and relating to the other players. The others include her in their scene without telling her what role she is expected to play. It is her challenge to figure out who they are, where they are, and who she is to be. This warm-up activity helps each player learn the process of listening, and of giving and taking focus on stage.

In *Fish Fiction,* the players think of one exotic fish and how it moves. One player is designated the "scene starter," in a group of no more than four players on stage. The players then begin to form strange and unusual movements, weaving in and out with one another, as they imagine their fish would. The leader "freezes" the action and the players hold their last position. The leader then points to one of the players and calls, "You are the 'scene starter.' Action!" The player who is designated the "scene starter" must decide what activity their position suggests and begin an improvised scene from that point. For example, bent over with the arms outstretched might suggest to the player to begin catching sand bags for stacking to prevent the river from flooding the town. The "scene starter" begins the action and dialogue and everyone else on stage responds in character to the person initiating the action.

THE ACTIVITY

Form a *body collage* or a stage picture based on a picture (a famous print or art painting, magazine picture, advertisement, *Sears* catalogue picture, historical event or current event). The players create an improvisation from the stage picture they have physically assembled. The players are learning to give and take the focus because the action and dialogue are not preset and must be spontaneous. The leader calls out "Action" to notify the players to begin and "Freeze" or "Curtain" to notify the players that their time is up and to again form the stage picture which began the scene.

VARIATIONS

In *Call Out The Characters,* a small group of five or six players creates spontaneous stage picture in which everyone is in physical contact with another person. The players change rapidly from one pose to another as the leader calls out characters. Some examples are: miners, soldiers, ballet dancers, rock singers, babies, teachers, actors, skiers, baseball players, tennis players, passengers on a sailboat, peo-

87

ple on a crowded elevator, king and queen and courtiers, the royal family, farmers, bull fighters, magicians, clowns, passengers waiting for the train, construction workers, circus performers, jazz musicians, disco dancers, teenie boppers, gamblers, cowboys, heads of state, politicians, sun bathers, druggies, participants at a stag party, company picnickers, football fans, research scientists, olympic athletes, astronauts, jailbirds, nuke protesters, carnival workers. Each player should be touching another, so that some part of each person's body is in physical contact with the whole. There are many levels on which each player can work: standing, sitting, crouching, reaching.

In *Reading Between the Lines,* four players are given a situation in which they are paired, where both pairs are given the circumstances (Who, What, Where, When and Why). One pair goes on stage while the remaining pair is part of the audience. The players in the audience become the voices of the actors on stage. The non-speaking players on stage act out the dialogue as it is spoken for them by the pair of voices in the audience. This activity requires a scene which has potential for physical activity, for example, a pregnant woman and her husband on the verge of delivery—she's calm and he's hysterical; a lifeguard saving the life of a non-swimmer; a mother and daughter (or father and son) in the anteroom just before a wedding.

For *Describe What's Next,* give several players on stage the outline of a scene (Who, What, Where, When and Why). As the players begin to improvise a scene, the leader calls out "Freeze," and a member of the audience instructs the actors on what is to happen next. The leader then calls "Action" and the players continue the scene as told by the audience.

WRAP-UP

As a completion to Stage II, your group may want to perform a photoplay. Use the photographs, stories and improvisations from *Living Snapshots, Magic Memories* and *The Tableaux* to create a photoplay. Photographs can easily be converted without much extra cost by following the simple process given here:

1. Obtain or borrow a 35 mm. camera.

2. Buy regular slide-colored film Ektachrome daylight 400. For this process, outside daylight is best so as not to create a glare. An overcast day is preferable, but not absolutely necessary.

3. Take your first picture and tape down its corners onto a flat surface (bulletin board, posterboard or cardboard). Stand up the surface so that it is vertical.

4. Place the camera so that the sun is in back of the camera, shining on the picture.

5. Hold the camera still, or place it on a surface level with the picture (example: tripod table or stool).

6. Look into the camera lens and make sure the entire photograph is framed and focused.

7. If your original picture is too small to fill the frame and maintain sharp focus, use a zoom lens. If you don't have a zoom lens, border the picture in black construction paper to avoid unsightly over-lappng of the picture with the surrounding border.

8. To make sure you get the best reproduction of old photographs, take three shots at different exposures. Take the first shot at the reading indicated by your light meter for this particular lighting situation. Take the next shot overexposing the film one f-stop and the last, underexposing the film one f-stop.

Once you have the photos ready, they can be used in the photoplay as background for demonstrating several of the activities described above. In *Living Snapshots* and *Magic Memories,* the players use photos to act out memories to which the audience can easily relate. In *The Tableaux,* the players use the photos as an instrument for creating a spontaneous improvisation. The photoplay may also be a Readers' Theatre performance accompanied by slides. The success of this photoplay is a good indication of the group's readiness for Stage III.

IDEAS FROM OTHER DIRECTORS

We have worked with guest artists on occasion, to give the group a different point of view, and to develop new approaches and skills. We have performed at several Illinois Theatre Association conventions and at the National Council on Aging Annual Conference, where we have had exciting interchange with others in the field of creative drama for senior adults. Here are a few secrets we've uncovered.

Bob Alexander, director of the Living Stage in Washington, had a special process for working through the emotions to become another character. He uses a relevant situation, such as the institutionalization of some older people. The players form two lines facing each other. One line represents the institutionalized. They each choose the individual impairments which brought them to the institution. The players in the other line are visitors to the institution. They must decide what their relationship is to the person opposite them, and what they are feeling about the visit. Each player is to discover as much as possible about the other person. The two players talk together within the character roles they have chosen.

After the players have talked and visited on a superficial level, have them, in turn, tell what they are really feeling, as if the other person were not there at all. Each player takes a turn telling his true feelings.

The leader plays the part of the owner of the institution. At some point, she informs the players that the institution will close at the end of the month and the residents will have to make other arrangements. The player residents then take time to talk with their visitor about what they are going to do—whether they will go to another institution or whether they will go home.

Direct the players to say good-bye, walking in slow motion back to the initial two lines from which they began. The players may think about a word that describes what they feel: fear, love, anger, frustration, peace. Let the feelings infuse their bodies. Each says his emotion word adding bodily expression. Each takes one step away from his partner and whispers the word.

The players in the group discuss what they discovered about themselves and the characters they represented. How did they choose who they were to be? How did they deal with the emotions of that character? How, if they had never been that person, did they know how to act like that character? Note the different disabilities and infirmities that were used and the variety of relationships.

The *Improvisational Olympics* was organized by David Shepherd, one of the founders of Compass Players, precursor to Second City. His interest was not in a finished performance, but in the creative process, and in bringing the audience into that process. From our participation in the Olympics, we adapted the following games to our needs as a group of older adults.

CHARACTER RELAY

The audience supplies the players with their identities and their relationships to each other. Each player chooses one physical prop such as a hat, newspaper, purse, umbrella, scarf, cane or broom, which helps him define his character. First, each player creates a story to play out with another player. When the leader calls, "Switch," this signals the switching of props and the switching of roles. This switching should take place several times during the course of the improvisation, without interrupting the action. When the leader calls out "Switch," the players take up where the other characters left off, as in a round-robin story. The players imitate as closely a possible the voice, body movement and attitude of the originating character.

WORKPUT

The audience supplies the players with a physical activity familiar to them, such as working out in a gym; sculpting in clay; cleaning the house; washing a car, or painting a room. It also supplies a topic to talk about which is unrelated to the work or activity the group is performing, such as politics, an argument with a loved one, an exciting date, a new friend, a boring party. At no point are the players to talk about the task they are doing. They are only to talk about the unrelated topic. *They must create a good idea of where they are and what they are doing without talking about it.* This is an excellent exercise for concentrating on stage. It is also good for pantomiming body movement, since the activity can only be seen in their actions. The players must keep their location continuously alive.

Working with guest artists, students, community theatre people, anyone with a fresh outlook, added to the fun and playfulness of the group.

Stage II is filled with many surprises. But most of all, it is filled with fun, laughter and the enjoyment of seeing the past come alive. Reliving moments of the past is a valuable tool for accepting ourselves and opening the door to the future. Up to this point the players have been sharing and creating a strong bond of camaraderie and ensemble spirit. If the players wish to move on, Stage II is a gentle transition into Stage III, the stage of performance.

Stage II is a place for letting go and beginning anew—letting go our fears of rejection and beginning to open ourselves up totally to the moment, the "Now." It is letting go of what journalist Ellen May Goldberg terms "hurry disease," and beginning to take time to listen to what we and other people are saying and doing. It is letting go of the rigid patterns of thinking and beginning to realize that two different viewpoints are only two ways of looking at a situation that has limitless possibilities for action and reaction. By the process of "letting go," we wind up in the end by getting it all together.

> Discovering ACTING UP! was like being given a golden key to a magic playground. I entered and suddenly I was doing things I had never dreamed I could do, finding new and different personalities in myself, living in a new world of my own creation.
>
> Birdell

STAGE III - TO PERFORM OR NOT TO PERFORM

> The only acting experience I've had was when I was in the third grade and had peanuts tied all over me, when I played the PEANUT MAN. When we first started rehearsals I felt like raw raw material. Now that we're performing I only feel like raw material. I'm going to give it a try.
>
> Tom Burns

We chose to perform, so that the players were able to share their experiences with others outside the group. The performance is a way of communicating our success to the community and to the organizations which sponsor us.

While you may not choose to have your group become a touring company, as we have, you will probably want to have at least one performance for the group's peers and family members. The group will most likely want to share its work with others. By giving at least one performance, it gives closure to your workshop activities and helps the participants realize that they have completed a worthwhile and significant experience.

After this, you may want to ask your members to see if they want to perform on a regular basis. The members might be more enthusiastic than you have anticipated and that will be the starting point for a "performance point of view." New considerations will have to be discussed.

PERFORMANCE CONSIDERATIONS

1. Listening. Because of difficulties with hearing, listening skills often need work. Listening becomes a problem in performance when actors fail to hear and respond to cues. Visual and physical cues often replace verbal cues: i.e., a touch on the shoulder or a loud musical instrument, preferably one with low frequency tones. (With hearing loss the high tones go first.) These serve as indicators of transitions in the scene. Some examples are: clapping, stomping one's feet, or striking the drum or claves. In the scripted scenes we incorporated visual cues into the blocking so that no one would feel anxious about missing his lines, even if he were unable to hear a spoken cue.

Discover each player's personal pathways to strong perception. Give directions slowly, clearly and concisely. It is beneficial to speak to the players individually or in small groups about details. Be willing to repeat and remember to take your time. It is helpful to write individual notes to members of the group. This allows each player to review his work independently. It is a good idea at the performance stage to have the players keep their directions in separate notebooks. These written notes help to get beyond the players' listening and hearing concerns.

2. Memory. "I thought I'd lost my memory, but now I'm finding it." Concern with memorization work often is not so much a disability as a skill which has been allowed to wither. Since there may be difficulty with a memorized script, we create our own material, which is easier to remember because it is ours. In order to play down many of the members' fears about memorization of lines we began evolving loose scripts through improvisations. The actors had to be "familiar and feel comfortable" with the lines of dialogue they had created, or to improvise a spontaneous script gathered from suggestions made by an audience. The players should be made aware that the more memorization they attempt, the more skillful they will become. With practice and encouragement, the members of ACTING UP! are improving greatly on remembering lines and cues.

Since you, as the leader, will be with the group for performances, you may become part of the show, either as the technical person (handing out props, running slides, playing music) or as a performer. In the performer capacity you can work with the audience before the show begins, warm up the players, or you can conduct a question-and-answer session at the end. As director you may become the narrator or emcee, tying all the pieces of the show together.

3. Attendance. There is a problem with regular attendance for the performance if the commitment is not made clearly at the beginning by

all of the members. Many elders are retired and are involved in a number of different activities which they choose. Conflicts will occur.

There is also the issue of illness. Rather than ignoring illness when putting together a show, create a format which is flexible, in which one person can easily take another's part and where the part can, if necessary, be eliminated without disturbing the format of the show.

4. *Weather and climate.* For many older adults the summer months are spent vacationing and being with family and friends. In the northern winter it becomes difficult to get around. Many of our members do not drive. The ones who do, don't like to drive in snowy weather. The overriding problem, however, is that half the troupe goes South for the depths of the winter. In Chicago, we find the most productive times for our group to meet and perform are in the spring and fall. This best serves our needs.

5. *Keeping men.* Statistically there are fewer older men. We have always had men in the troupe, but it has been somewhat of a problem keeping them from year to year. At least half of the original members of ACTING UP! are still performing and they are all women. A number of men have participated for a while and then have left at the end of a season. They usually have other activities and ACTING UP! becomes less important as other activities take over their lives. At the present we have three men actively performing with the group and another participates when he is able.

Since we do not have tryouts and we are most anxious to retain and encourage men to participate, we are very flexible about allowing new members to enter the group. In our fourth performing season, a new energetic enthusiastic man wanted to become part of the group. He was able to attend rehearsals and performances, but as time went on it became obvious that he was unable to accommodate himself to the needs and goals of the group. He constantly added new "bits" to his part which were not checked out with the leader and began to tell everyone else what to do. We began work on a new scripted piece and he became very critical of others and would not stick to the script. Several members of the group were so annoyed that they were about to quit. It was the leader's responsibility at that point to decide whether to keep him and try to adjust to his ways, or to ask him to leave. In the interests of the group, which had been ongoing for several years, it was decided that we could not risk breaking it apart for one person. Sadly, we had to ask him to leave.

6. *Rigidity.* Many people come to the group with certain rigid attitudes and are very skeptical of many of the things we are doing. Usually by the time the performance stage is reached, these people will have taken backstage roles or have left the group entirely. But in case you get a new player after the performance is set, you should be aware that it may take that person some time to let go and "go with the flow." Usually all the experienced members will assist in orientation of a new member and turn fear to joyful experience, the new member becoming totally committed to the group.

7. *Socializing or Rehearsing.* There is a tendency to socialize at the beginning of each session instead of getting down to work. Socialization needs to be somewhat limited so that the show can be well rehearsed. A good method of dealing with the need for socialization is to organize an exciting, fun warm-up at the beginning of each rehearsal, so that everyone feels energized and connected to the ensemble. Use the activities from Stages I and II, as well as those given for Stage III.

8. *Equality.* Older people have a wide variety of skills, functional intelligence levels, physical abilities and talents which run the gamut even though the people are similar in age. Therefore, as the leader recognizes who has what skills, she should capitalize on those strong points which are obvious to the group and challenge other areas which she sees as strong performance values. She tries to let all the members contribute their ideas to make all the players feel that they have an investment in the performance. It is a collaborative process, a democratic system in which everyone has an equal voice. Equal performing time is not always possible, but contributions of equal value are.

9. *Sharing the responsibility.* In the performance stage the responsibilities of the leader begin to grow. It is good at this point to delegate some responsibilities to members of the group. Another way to broaden the base of the group for support when performing is by finding teenagers, college students, community theatre people and others to volunteer their time and support to performing with the group and helping with some of the responsibilities. If you choose to tour, you, as leader, will need to strengthen your position as artistic director to be able to guide the quality of the performance and work more closely with the players. You need to be able to refine your concentration specifically to the performance. In order to do this, you will need a Business Manager to make bookings, follow up communications, make media contacts, send out and collect evaluations and assist in funding proposals. This member may come from the group, the community or the sponsoring organization.

10. *Transportation.* This becomes a concern if you take your performance on tour. When we first began performing at different locales, everyone drove cars or car-pooled. Often there was tardiness or confusion. We now have an official van or bus which everyone meets at an appointed time and regular place. It returns everyone to the same spot, from which the players are responsible for finding a way home. In most areas transportation of this type (van, bus or station wagon) is available, often free-of-charge, through community, arts or elders' organizations.

We have developed the process geared to changes. Any group which stays together long enough is bound to change. As leader you continually adapt to your group's needs and lifestyles for an ongoing, expansive experience.

THE RAINBOW DEVICE

Through the ACTING UP! process we solve problems by making the problems part of the process. As in the play *Vanities,* where the audience views the actors putting on their make-up, the ACTING UP! players let themselves be seen as people as well as performers. The players become graceful enough so that when something happens during a performance (for example, someone gets the giggles, forgets a line, can't move) it becomes part of the performance. The players may show their struggling, but that is part of the humanity of the group. The show will work no matter what happens.

During one performance piece we developed what we call the *Rainbow Device.* One player has a line that goes, "You see this blouse? It has many, many colors: blue, red, yellow and green. In fact, it reminds me of a rainbow. Who knows, someday I might reach the end of the rainbow and find a pot of gold. I can dream, can't I?" We came up with the *Rainbow Device* when this player continually went blank on the word "rainbow." She would say it reminds me of a "_____" and go blank. All the other players supported her, saving the stage moment by saying in choral style, "Rainbow." She would continue on as if it were part of the play. Eventually this small awkward moment grew into a spontaneous stage device that we continue to call upon in any similar situation.

Thus the group has developed a spirit of ensemble so that when a player makes a mistake the others can pick up and go on. Another example of creative problem-solving occurred when a player was portraying a retired senior citizen who was actively pursuing those things he never had time to do before retirement. He jogged for seven minutes on stage while the rest of the skit was taking place around him. By the time the players got to the finale, he was supposed to be out of breath, which he was. During one performance the audience ap-plauded his seven minute effort. This took him off guard and he momentarily blanked out on what he was supposed to say. Realizing that he forgot his opening line, he improvised and said:

> You know sometimes we forget our lines, but since the important thing is that we are up here on stage impro-vising about our own lives, I don't feel badly about forgetting my lines. I forgot my lines because I was excited, not because I'm over sixty-five and can't re-member something for very long. This is real life. I am playing me, not a role, and I'd just like to say that I was so excited to see you and receive your warm response that I forgot my lines. I really am jogging through my retirement years.

The last line he said was received so well by the cast and audience that it has remained in the performance ever since. Every mistake can be turned into an advantage. Being able to deal with problems in a creative way turns the players' mistakes into accomplishments. "If you're lucky to find a group like this, you feel like you're a giant step ahead of everyone else if you keep on ACTING UP!"

READERS' THEATRE
TECHNIQUES FOR PERFORMANCE

Your goals for a touring performance may include mounting both improvised vignettes and the players' written dramatic pieces. Read-ers' Theatre is an excellent transition between theatre games and writing activities, and fully staged performance. In Readers' Theatre the players can perform seated or standing; they do not have to memorize; they read from a script; and they are able to work from their collection of personal writings in a performance.

Readers' Theatre can be a powerful theatre form. It need not be overlooked as less important than another method of performance. The only technical aspect you may wish to use to enhance the performance is stage lighting which will help set a mood and give focus to the performers.

Readers' Theatre relies heavily on vocal skills. The following exercises isolate and develop skills necessary for players who choose to perform for an audience with Readers' Theatre.

Breathing

Stable breath control to support performance speaking requires breathing from the diaphragm. Locate your diaphragm by standing in front of a mirror and placing your hands on your lower, side ribs; then fill your lungs with air. Notice the expansion of your abdomen and lower ribs. Continue to breathe deeply without moving your shoulders up and down, using only the lower (diaphragm) muscles. Sense the action on your belt as you take sharp, short breaths from deep in your abdomen. Call "Hhheelllooooo!" as if standing on one mountain, communicating to a player on another mountain. Call "Hello" again, this time opening your mouth first slightly, then normally, then wide. What differences do you notice in yourself and in other players in the way "Hello" is said?

Articulation

In order to sharpen consonants and extend vowels, players pair up and speak to one another, first stressing consonants and then stressing vowels. One sentence may be used, "Please go to the store and buy me seven dollars of cat food," or, players may take turns engaging in everyday conversation while the leader calls out "Consonants," then "Vowels." Players stress the called-for sounds as they speak. Pay particular attention to the final consonants in each word, and stress the final consonant of each sentence.

Tongue-twisters are excellent tools for developing better articulation. Some examples include phrases and nonsense-words like, "Putika, Putika, Putika," "The lips, the teeth, the tip of the tongue," "She sells sea shells by the sea shore," "Peter Piper picked a peck of pickled peppers...," Say these first slowly and with careful articulation, and then as fast as you can, crisply clipping the consonants.

For fun and variety in vocal exercises, try practicing articulation on "The Jabberwocky," from *Alice in Wonderland:*

'Twas brillig, and the slithy toves
Did gyre and gimble in the wabe!
All mimsy were the borogoves
And the mome raths outgrabe...

Or, practice rapid, precise articulation on one of Gilbert and Sullivan's patter songs, like "Modern Major General;"

I am the very model of a modern major general.
I've information; vegetable, animal and mineral.
I know the kings of England and I quote the
fights historical
From Marathon to Waterloo in order categorical...

Other Vocal Elements

Pitch. Talk to each other, repeating the same or similar thoughts in high and low tones. Note the differing emotional qualities conveyed by changes in pitch. Which sounds more authoritative? Which more helpless?

Projection. Projection includes volume, but means the ability to speak to listeners at chosen distances, e.g., addressing someone three feet away with the same emotional content as someone across the room or at the back of the auditorium. Speak intimately to people at various distances. Then, speak boldly to these same people. Notice the extra pressure on your belt, as you speak intimately to someone far away. Breath control pays off in this exercise. Actors on tour in a play make good use of their skills in projection as they move into varying-sized auditoriums from week to week, but must present the same emotional content to their audiences in these differing spaces.

Quality or texture. Try out some variety in your vocal texture: Nasal, throaty, scratchy, smooth, breathy, husky, breathless. Do these differing sounds remind you of different people you know? Texture is one identifying trait of characters you may play. Notice how skilled impressionists vary the texture of their voices to imitate famous characters. Changes in texture are subtle; if you try to imitate Louis "Satchmo" Armstrong for long, your throat will hurt.

Intensity and nuance. Using the phrase, "I won't!" vary the intensity of expression and note the results. For example, you could put a lot of energy into a whisper, or make a flaccid scream.

Tempo and meter. Think of the pace at which the syllables fly by. Tempo is more than speed of speech. For example, ordinary Spanish sounds rapid when compared to English. Part of the appearance of speed lies in the number of stressed syllables in a given sentence. "Over the river and through the woods," sounds faster than, "The ship went sailing o'er the sea."

Try saying the same short speech at sixty words per minute, and then at 190 words per minute. Note the tendency to emphasize consonants at the faster rate, and vowels at the slower pace. How does tempo affect regional dialect?

Pauses. Pauses are used for emphasis. Recite this speech with, and then without, a pause. "I'm going on vacation. I'm going to New York. (pause) I have a friend there. S/he's an interior decorator!" Notice the difference in meaning between the two readings.

Non-verbal Communication

Gibberish. Gibberish is defined here as meaningless word-sounds. Sid Caesar speaks in gibberish when he plays a caveman. He tells a story, and everyone understands him, but the words are an unknown language. People understand him through gestures and facial expression. The meaningless words provide emphasis.

Try a gibberish game for three. The first person leaves the room, while the second tells the third a story in gibberish. Number One re-enters and Three tells her the same story in gibberish, trying to copy as faithfully as possible Number Two's sounds, gestures and expressions. Finally, Number One relates the story in English, to see how close to the original he was able to understand it. Practice in gibberish strengthens the players' ability to communicate with more than words.

Posture. Take note of your posture when you speak in anger; in sympathy; in jest; in resignation; in defiance.

Eye contact. It is difficult to maintain, but essential when performing Readers' Theatre. Try standing in front of the room, holding eye contact for a full minute with someone, without speaking. Then try reading a short speech to the group, maintaining as much eye contact as possible.

Speech elicits movement

Gestures and body movement may come from speech. Tensions arise in your body when you speak. When you vary the pitch, intensity and volume of your voice, your body reacts to the variations with changes in posture, activity and position.

Certain words or sentences seem to cry out for body movements. Try speaking and letting your body move with the following short sentences; play with sound values and gestures while saying, "I'm tired!" "Hello, Kitty Cat," "Pass the butter," and, "Treat me well, or you'll wish you had!"

DAILY DRILL

Here is a "daily half-dozen" exercises you may use to keep in shape vocally when the emphasis is on other acting skills:

1. Sip breath slowly—spreading your ribs, and hold your breath for five counts; then exhale, counting as high as you can. Try to keep your ribs extended, and breathe only from the diaphragm. Pant like a dog and feel the action on your belt.

2. Count to five aloud, stressing on each sequence, one through five, the next number, i.e., **1**, 2, 3, 4, 5; 1, **2**, 3, 4, 5. Push the numbers out of your stomach in short, staccato bursts.

3. Laugh, "Ho, ho, ha, ha, hi, hi." Pause an instant between each sound and feel your stomach tighten on each explosive sound.

4. Call out military-like commands:
"Left, right, *left,* right." (Part of the time emphasize *"Right."*)
"On your mark. Get set. Go!"
"Back to the road, *all of you!"*

5. Call, using long vowels and deep diaphragm support.
"Wherefore rejoice, you blocks, you stones, you worse-than-senseless things. *Begone!"*
"Apples, potatoes, watermelons!"
"Okay, Joe..let 'er go! OK, Bill...Take 'em away!"

6. Emotions: See how many ways you can say the word or phrase.
"Yes" or "No."
"But, I can't."
"We have to go."

Choral Reading

Echoing another player's words emphasizes important words in a script. Practice saying words like "No, yes, lonely, happy" together as a group. Several players repeat the word "love" in rapid succession, each echoing the person before him.

The following piece is an example of Readers' Theatre material, complete with director's notes.

CHILDHOOD MEMORIES
by Mary Kerr Smith

(Said in an excited childlike voice)

Often the memory comes to me of the sleepy little town I lived in as a child *(all performers yawn and stretch)*, the clay driveway up to the house where I first took off my shoes and socks and waded in the puddles after a rain *(the performers make the sound of rain)*, and caught sand-itch *(the players wiggle their feet)*, a troublesome thing that strikes newcomers to Florida, not the natives. Mother bathed and bandaged for weeks and out of that came the dictum: *(spoken chorally)* "Barefeet only in the house!"

And there was "Aunt Alice" who'd weathered some eighty-seven years when we first met. I was six. She was originally from Chicago. *(The players sing, "Chicago, Chicago, that toddlin' town.")* We spent Sunday afternoons together listening to the Victrola while the great, soaring voice of Caruso came through *(in opera-like voice, one performer sings a note)*, and Schumann Heinck *(another player sings another note)* and Galli Curci *(a third player sings another note)*, or the laughing songs of "Uncle Josh" *(all the performers laugh)*, or the Scottish songs of heather and kilt by Harry Lauder.

Aunt Alice had a Sesame box of "jewels," pearls and beads *(all the players make an awed "oh" sound as if seeing a magnificent treasure)*. She let me dress up her hair with them.

Then there was the time I took my red raincoat and demonstrated how Rudolph Valentino fought the bull *(the group calls out chorally, "Olé!" "Olé!" "Olé!")*, the bull being Malcolm, a young calf she had *(everyone "moos")*. I felt daring and she enjoyed it so much. Malcolm just looked as if to say, "What's this all about?" and calmly chewed on a piece of straw *(everyone makes exaggerated wide-eyed chewing movements)*, wide-eyed and wondering.

ENSEMBLE SPIRIT

In preparation for the performance we use activities which assist a group of players, to share focus and support one another as the need arises. The following are activities geared to the fun and freedom found in working together as a group.

Telling a story round-robin with everyone taking a part helps the players to participate in the spirit of the ensemble. Begin a theme such

as "I went to the academy awards ceremony...." Each person in turn continues the story until each player has had the opportunity to contribute. In order to make the story cohesive, the players must go beyond their thoughts to hear how the story develops and what the other person is saying.

This group collaboration can expand story-telling into poetry-writing, in *The Poem Song*. Offer an idea for a group poem, for example, "Now that it's spring, it's a wonderful thing." While the leader sings a theme to a made-up tune, anyone in the group can call out a word, a thought or a phrase that is associated with the initial idea. For example, "My tulips are blooming, the birds are on the wing;" "The sky is blue;" "God's in heaven and all's right with the world;" "Rabbits are jumping." It does not have to rhyme or be metaphorical. It can be anything that comes to mind about the particular theme being used.

When a player calls out an idea the group stops and listens. Then the leader begins to sing her phrase, "Now that it's spring, it's a wonderful thing," over and over again until someone else speaks up. It is beneficial to tape-record this activity and listen to it after you feel you have enough material from the majority of the group. Possible themes are: courage, love, freedom, grandchildren, children, justice and the seasons.

ACTING UP! players performed this activity around the theme, "Over sixty-five makes me glad to be alive," and each player made it his own by singing any of the words in any sequence with any rhythm or any tune. All the players participated at the same time. Just as jazz musicians improvise with their instruments, we encouraged spontaneous vocal improvisation around a theme.

We used "Over 65 makes us glad to be alive" as an audience warm-up (having the audience chant along with us) and as an exit line. We then decided to incorporate it into the beginning of the show. Each person introduced himself to the audience with a four-line original poem, stating his name, age and something significant about himself. Once the players all introduced themselves and formed a stage picture, they chorally chanted:

> We all like to ACT UP
> On performing we all thrive
> It makes us feel that youthful glow
> Though we're over sixty-five, over sixty-five,
> over sixty-five.
> Over sixty-five makes us glad to be alive!
> Over sixty-five makes us glad to be alive!

The vitality of raising one's voice in song without worrying about being on key or in time is a great release of inhibitions. This freeing-up of feelings within the group allows the ensemble spirit to grow, nurtured by laughter and zest.

All of the activities in Stages I and II have been developed for the creation of performance vignettes and character studies. It is important to repeat these activities with rehearsals in order to discover new qualities about familiar characters from previous improvisations. We have not repeated those here, but, instead, have selected specific exercises designed to be used as an extension of the previous activities.

The following activities at one time or another have been developed into performance pieces for our touring company repertoire. The only thing that separates these spontaneous improvisation exercises from more polished pieces are rehearsals. The basic structure of our performance is implicit in all the theatre games we experience.

The more rehearsals an activity receives, the more polished it becomes. Balanced with our rehearsed work are spontaneous improvisations which keep our performances and players ever new, exciting and vital.

GETTING INTO CHARACTER

An activity geared to examining different characters is entitled *Getting Into Character*. This exercise helps the players to see how it feels to be another character.

The players pick anyone they know, past or present, personal or fictional. They may pick the fictional character from something they have read: a novel, short story or play. Each player may use the following form and shares aloud the answers with the rest of the group.

Vital Statistics: Age_____Weight_____

Color of eyes_____

Hair Color_____Height_____

Married_____Single_____

How many children_____

Describe the kinds of clothes the character normally wears.

Where and in what kind of house does the character live?

Describe the personality of the character.

If the character had a flat tire in the middle of the night, what would this person do?

How does the character act in an argument?

What does the character want? Need? What is at stake?

If the character were a criminal, what kind of crime would he commit?

What is your character's favorite joke?

What is your character's Invested Object?

What does your character have in his pocket or her purse?

Who is your character's favorite person?

What is his biggest secret? Greatest fear? Favorite fantasy?

Who does this character care about? How is this affection shown?

Now that you have all this information, see how close the players can come to impersonating the character. For fifteen minutes to a half hour have the players become that person. Have the players describe what they did, how they felt, what changes they had to make in their ways of thinking and moving. After they have explored this character alone, the players pair up. Through the combination of their characters, have them create a situation with a conflict and a resolution, then play it on stage.

THE DRAMATIC TRAP

A performance based on improvisation works best for ACTING UP! We get a lot of our material for the improvisational shows from the activity entitled *The Dramatic Trap*. Two people in small group improvisations lead to larger scenes involving the entire troupe. *The Dramatic Trap* improvisation brings characters from all backgrounds together in an uncommon situation from which they cannot escape.

Circumstances which might lend themselves to this *Dramatic Trap* situation are: a bus load of strangers trapped in a diner by a snow storm, a class reunion, a cruise ship, an airplane, a wedding, bleachers at a ballgame, night school, or an all-night diner.

The players can choose from a variety of characters: weight lifters, priests, English teacher, nun, politician, rabbi, shopping-bag lady, karate teacher, taxi driver—a few of many possibilities. The players are encouraged to play a wide-range of roles which will stretch their skills and reveal new parts of themselves. Because opposite roles are contained within our complex human natures, playing roles we wouldn't ordinarily choose in daily life broadens our perspective about the possibilities for growth and self-understanding.

After the players on stage know who and where they are, the leader introduces the *Dramatic Trap,* which is a situation and a place where the characters must stay and solve their problems collectively. *The Howard Street El* (see Appendix) was developed into a scripted play from this activity.

Here are some ideas for light-hearted *Dramatic Trap* combinations:

1. Exercise class for sixties and over.

2. A retired singles club.

3. A meeting of overeaters anonymous.

4. A family reunion/old feud is dug up.

5. Shopping at a grocery store.

6. Babysitting with grandchildren whom grandma and grandpa fear are devils.

7. A visit to the doctor—everyone is complaining of ailments.

8. A Bar Mitzvah or Confirmation celebration.

9. A play rehearsal with a new understudy or prima donna.

DEVELOPING IMPROVISATION
FOR PERFORMANCE

PROPS AS MOTIVATION

"Motivation stimulus" develops the character's reasons for an action. Motivation can come through the use of props. Put together a collection of props such as old shoes, pots and pans, gloves, a metronome, a book, a hubcap, a rope, a tennis racket. Divide the players into small groups and have each group select one or two of the props. Once they have made the selection, they create a scene in which the prop (or props) become the central motivating element. The prop will generate the idea of the *what*. (See Stage II - Role Playing for Element of Character) They will then need to decide on the *who* and the *where*. Using a prop for motivation stimulus provides the scene with action and energy.

Put together a collection of hats from the players' attics or garage sales. Put the variety of hats on the floor and encourage each player to choose a hat. Once the players have chosen their hats, have them think about what kind of character might wear that hat. When they each have a character in mind, you can match them up in pairs or triads and let them create the scene. They begin with the *who* and then have to decide on the *where* and the *what*.

One day in rehearsal, a doll, which was someone else's prop for another vignette, was lying on stage. Flo picked it up and decided on the spur of the moment that she was going to create the character of a young woman who got into "trouble" and was left without her man, but burdened with a child. Another character joined her scene as an on-the-street TV interviewer. The scene grew, becoming humorous, poignant and human. After this any kind of prop or costume part left on stage was an invitation to the players to develop spontaneous "free play" improvisations.

ENVIRONMENT AS MOTIVATION

The players use sensory recall to project the environment to the audience by their subtle reactions to different types of weather, time of day and the actual locale of the scene.

An activity geared to sensory recall of an environment takes the players along a journey through unusual environments. The players walk around the playing area as if they are walking through peanut butter, jello, four-foot snow drifts, marshmallows, hot sand, cool pebbly creek, bubble gum, a dense dark jungle. Now take the players through another image walk, where they act out different images, connected to the various seasons, combining sensory recall and body movement:

SPRING—climb a tree, play a game of tennis, plant a garden, become a blooming flower.

SUMMER—swim through the water, become the waves of the ocean, mow the lawn, row a boat.

FALL—walk through crisp air and crunchy leaves, become the leaves falling, rake the leaves, pick apples.

WINTER—skate outdoors in a park, ski on the slopes of Aspen, become snowflakes, shovel snow, become a tree in a blizzard.

Using the environment as motivation also involves the creative use of space. In these exercises use a tambourine as a rhythm-controlling agent or as a textured background. Ask the group to use the whole space effectively, making sure not to bump into another person. Have them be aware of their individual space and its relation to the larger space. Ask them to maintain eye contact as much as they can with other persons they pass.

Variations can be: Walking, slow motion, fast motion, freezing and shaking the hand of the person closest to you, freezing and giving a stroke or compliment to a person, walking backwards or sideways, walking as monsters or animals without bumping or touching another person, walking as the other sex. Another space situation concerns moving about in a crowd situation, such as a rock concert, bargain basement, or political rally. An outgrowth of the walking exercise would be to play tag with one person being "it."

Create a Space. You may want to combine a theme suggested in a previous activity with a new setting to create a space. You can create the *where* with available props or set pieces or from imagination. Keep the focus on objects around you. Show who you are through contact with the immediate environment. Decide on where the scene takes place: a jail, a dungeon, a cellar, a cave, a boxcar, a hospital room, a bedroom, a mine, an attic, a tower, a church steeple, a tree house, a cocktail lounge, a greasy spoon restaurant, a dining room, a dentist's office, a library, a church, a drug store.

Soundscape. Make a sound tape, using voices to create sounds for a particular environment: jungle, the moon, turkish bath, motel, school, high-rise apartment building, subway station. After listening to the tape, decide what is happening in the environment and create scenes suggested by its sounds. You may choose to use the sound tape as a backdrop for acting out the scene.

109

A good example of this activity is "Sounds of the City of Yesteryear." Think back to the city and the advent of the automobile, when life felt different and the city was the place you called home. Imagine the sounds of your city and recreate those sounds individually or in groups—horses' hooves (clip-clopping), street vendors ("Rags and old irons! Tomatoes! Watermelons! Fish for sale!"), newspaper boy ("Extra! Extra! Read all about it!"), the horns of the automobiles (ahoogah, ahoogah!) the clang-a-langing of the streetcar and the screech of the jitney wheels.

When we did this exercise a performance piece developed called "Do You Remember?" As we were recalling the sounds of the city we began to recall other incidents out of the past and "the way things used to be."

Do you remember when all your doctors were older than you?

Do you remember the crash, when one day we ate chicken and the next day we ate the feathers?

Do you remember the hot summer nights that you, your family and neighbors slept out in the park or on the fire escape?

Do you remember binding your chest or oiling your pompadour hairdo?

Do you remember "spooning" in the rumble seat?

Do you remember summer evenings on the front porch swing?

Do you remember the street entertainers: the stilt walkers, the trained bear, and the monkey organ grinder, and the man who tap-danced for pennies and nickles?

Do you remember unbuckled galoshes and the sound they made as you walked through the snow?

Concerns of aging can lend themselves to improvisations and discoveries of strong feelings leading to possible solutions. Some ideas in this area are:

1. Mandatory retirement, pro or con.

2. Physical changes of the body.

3. Loss of senses or fears of loss.

4. Sex after sixty.

5. Isolation imposed on older adults by younger people.

6. Life on a tight budget.

7. Gaining or maintaining weight.

8. Loneliness—how to spend one's time alone.

9. Special diets and how to maintain them.

10. Relationships with offspring—trust and mistrust.

11. Doctors who don't take your medical concerns seriously.

12. Living in the past as an obsession—fear of present and future.

While the leader may suggest several problems, let the group invent most of the ideas. They will dream up problems which affect them. The group will discuss some of these concerns from time to time, not only toward creating an improvisation, but as experience-sharing and emotional release when needed.

PROVERBS STIMULATE IMPROVISATION

Talk about some of the proverbs we have carried with us from childhood on. Make up a list of proverbs. Divide the players into small groups and assign each one a proverb to act out with dialogue. The audience is to guess what the proverb is at the end of the scene. Some suggestions for proverbs are:

1. Haste makes waste.

2. Life begins at forty.

3. Too many cooks spoil the broth.

4. Children should be seen and not heard.

5. Charity begins at home.

6. One rotten apple spoils the whole barrel.

7. A woman's place is in the home.

8. An ounce of prevention is worth a pound of cure.

9. Into each life a little rain must fall.

10. You win some and you lost some.

11. Once bitten, twice shy.

12. A stitch in time saves nine.

This motivation stimulus is a good one because it gives the players the theme and encourages humor and ensemble spirit.

A good variation involves advertisements from newspapers or magazines. Have everyone bring in ads from newspapers and magazines with catchy slogans. You can either use the visual ad as a tableau (see Stage II Living Snapshots) in which a small group begins and ends a scene as the characters in the ad. Or you can take the slogans and assign them to small groups and have the players act them out. Obvious and well-known ad slogans such as "You've come a long way, baby!" or "You deserve a break today," lend themselves to audience participation improvisations. After the vignette, the audience tries to guess which slogan has been acted out. You can use headlines from magazine or newspaper articles as a motivation stimulus for improvisation.

Another variation is *Dear Abby*. Have everyone bring in her favorite *Dear Abby* letter and read it to the group. Select the best letters (the ones which are most humorous or have interesting characters) and assign them to small groups of two or three. Have them create the scene which led up to the writing of the letter, ending the scene with the reading of the letter to the audience.

Still another variation involves the use of problems or conflicts that need resolving since these form the heart of drama. Get a variety of ideas from your group for problems or conflicts which might make an exciting scene. Select the best ones to assign to the small groups. They will create the *who, where and what* of the scene. Suggestions for problems and conflicts are:

1. Locked out of a room in a motel—no extra key.

2. Teacher in a classroom unable to keep order.

3. Boss firing an employee from a job after many years of work.

4. On a date—telling the boyfriend you are pregnant.

5. Stuck in an elevator—nobody comes to the rescue.

6. Waiting for a job interview—discovering you're in the wrong place.

7. Waiting in a doctor's office for a long time—the nurse announces the doctor has been called away for surgery.

PREPARING FOR PERFORMANCE

How do we organize the program so that it satisfies an audience? Knowing what engages the audience means using the group's good experiences. Because elders carry a rich repertoire of memories, we can recapture these emotional and experiential moments and put them into dramatic form. As we work through a variety of improvisational experiences, we try to seize the best moments. That is, we hold onto scenes or dramatic incidents that played well in rehearsal, and refashion these for performance, whether it be *Oral History, The Machine* or an improvisation developed from the *Dramatic Trap* activity.

It is a good idea to evaluate possible performance material with a more critical eye than has been expected up until now. In preparation for a performance that works well for an audience, a good list of questions should now be used on all activities and rehearsals.

1. What worked well? Why? What could have played better? How?

2. Did the players effectively use voice, body and imagination in creating and projecting their roles?

3. Could you hear what was being said?

4. Did the players commit themselves to their part? Did you believe their interpretation?

5. Were the players listening to each other?

6. What suggestions do you have for the players in the scene? How would you like it to end?

The real test of audience appeal is performing before a variety of groups to see which parts of the show are most successful. Keeping in mind that audiences are as different and unique as individuals, we have changed our material so that the show appeals to a wide variety of audiences.

During the creation of the improvisations, members of the troupe get instant feedback from other members. In that way they begin to know the effectiveness of their work. The leader's encouragement helps to maintain the creative free-flow of ideas, which can be organized and given shape later. During the performance the players receive instant feedback from the audience, so that, if something needs strengthening, it can be easily adjusted. Each performance, then, is a collaborative effort. Every member of the group has contributed his input: ideas, writing, criticism, re-writing and creativity.

TO PERFORM

I wanted to die at sixty-nine so I would not have to go
through the physical pain of aging, but now after
seeing ACTING UP!, I am not so sure about that.
A Young Audience Member

We have developed versions of stimulating theatre games geared to
the special interests and needs of older adults. The improvisational
form serves us well in creating new dramatic works that serve the
troupe and enlighten its audiences as to the changing images of aging:

1. by presenting an image of vital, exciting seniors and

2. by performing provocative material, shattering the stereotypes
and myths of ageism.

We base all ACTING UP! performances on improvisations set by
group agreement into repeatable performance scenes. All the material,
therefore, is written or created by the performers themselves, with
guidance from the leader.

The leader may give each person a prop, a situation, or some other
idea to stimulate creativity, but the group members work out the
situations from their experiences and imaginations. When the players
create the situations or the dialogue, they will be able to recall these
lines more readily. They will have more of an emotional stake in the
production.

Ultimately the performance is no longer improvisation. It becomes
a rehearsed and set piece. A script may be written word for word or
simply outlined. Lines may change slightly over time and new
approaches to an incident tried. In this way the performance evolves
and deepens, and the performers' confidence grows.

We begin the ACTING UP! performance with music, since it ener-
gizes the performers and stimulates the audience. The following are
examples of some possible performance pieces that could be undertaken.

"Those Were The Days"* is a good musical vehicle. Since the
players had developed the knack of both physical and verbal improvisations, several members wanted to bring in some form of music. We
decided to begin the program with an acapella group performance of

---

* "Those Were the Days," Gene Raskin (New York: Essex Music,
Inc., 1968)

"Those Were the Days," using rhythm instruments. (This plan suited the troupe well, as there were at that time no skilled musicians among us.) The second verse was changed to "These Are the Days" to alert the audience that elders not only think about days gone by, but are thinking and acting in the present, and of how they can make the present more interesting and fulfilling.

> Those were the days, my friend
> We thought they'd never end
> We'd sing and dance forever and a day.
>
> We'd live the life we'd choose
> We'd fight and never lose,
> For we were *young* and sure to have our way.
> La, la, la, la, la, la,
> La, la, la, la, la, la
> Those were the days,
> Oh, yes, those were the days.
>
> These are the days, my friend
> We hope they'll never end
> We'll sing and dance forever and a day.
> We'll live the life we choose
> We'll fight and never lose
> For we are *strong* and sure to have our way.
> La, la, la, la, la, la,
> La, la, la, la, la, la
> Those were the days,
> Oh, yes, these are the days.

Look At Me is a presentation of self. Each performer takes center stage to tell the audience why she is wearing a particular color shirt or tunic, and how that color says something about who and what she is. Each person chooses a vivid color—one which says something about her identity and scotches the myth of drabness about elders. Since older adults are often "in the back of the bus," this puts them in the spotlight.

The Young Part of Me presents some aspect of each person which is forever young, despite the outward "physical overcoat" or appearance. In some of our early discussions many members acknowledged that even though they might look older to the world, they always felt young inside. They were wearing the costumes of age, but the personal actions and thoughts, or personality, of each was still whatever her

115

favorite age might be. We decided that each person would tell the audience about the part of her which is "young" and always will be. "The young part of me is: Snow on the roof, but fire in the furnace!"

Geriatric Jeans pokes fun with exaggerated humor at "youth cult" biases in popular advertising. One of the members does a "Brooke Shields" imitation demonstrating jeans:

Senior Citizen: I'm making money by modeling jeans. Every time there's a commercial, I get paid.

Interviewer: You don't look anything at all like Brooke Shields. What kind of jeans do you model?

Senior Citizen: Why, I model the Geritol Jeans, designed for senior seats, by Granny Goose. These pants are especially made to fit the relaxed rump, the sagging seat. They're made with safety in mind.

Interviewer: What's safety got to do with a pair of jeans?

Senior Citizen: D'ever hear of older people falling and breaking a hip? Not when you're wearing the Geritol Jeans, no sir! Why, Granny Goose jeans won't let you fall! They're so tough and rugged, so stiff that they stand up straight, even though you start to bend over. That's right, they wait for you to come back up! They hold you up. Try Geritol Jeans, designed by Granny Goose, and live an upright life.

From this poke at the youth-oriented commercials of the present, we got the idea of creating more satirical versions of commercials that we remembered from the past—either on TV or radio. We then talked about present-day commercials promoting products for older adults which we might present as further commentary on the stereotypes (especially in the media) of ageism.

Senior Secrets (see Appendix) was inspired by a lecture given by Maggie Kuhn, the leader of the Gray Panthers. She stated that eventually aging will get the respect it deserves and it will be rather chic to be a senior citizen. We decided to reverse some of the typical responses to aging, and designed an "advertisement" for "Senior Secrets"—with sequined liver spots, add-on wrinkles as beauty aids instead of false eyelashes and Oil of Olay. One of the company members wrote a commercial for beauty aids for the "mature" woman of the future.

Through humor, this piece gives the audience and the company a chance to laugh and look at some of the ways older people are discriminated against within the culture. It breaks some of the isolation that attitudes about aging cause, and somehow ameliorates the pain and self-consciousness and allows us to think about aging from a fresh and humorous perspective.

We Ought to Be in Pictures presents slides (photos) with comments from each performer. It begins with some group photos, then goes on to feature each of the members of the ensemble with photos from his past—baby pictures, pictures from youth with mates, and present photos, ending with some group photos of past ACTING UP! shows and rehearsal activities.

This part of the program has excited our audiences—particularly younger ones—because it reveals clearly that these people in front of them once were young, and illustrates how they have passed through various stages of life. It says, "Don't believe that the person you see in front of you is the only 'me.' I am who I was, who I am, and what I will be. I am the evolution of a human being."

COSTUMES

Since many touring companies have special T-shirts as identifying costumes and to give a unified look, we needed to find something comparable. One of our players bought materials in different patterns and textures and fashioned a tunic for each woman, which displays the "Look at Me" colors symbolic of that person. The men wear solid color shirts. On the tunics and shirts we pin a large badge with the name, ACTING UP!

Many of the older adults keep hats and clothes from their past. In a scene entitled "Grab Bag History," we conceived of the idea of bringing in hats and clothes from other eras (30's, 40's, 50's, 60's). We throw them all together and everyone dives into the pile and tries on the clothes, trying to get articles of clothing from several of the eras (like playing dress-up). This creates an interesting visual effect for the audiences and gives spirit and energy to the performers. The incongruity of a variety of styles worn side by side adds a touch of humor as we are literally wearing our memories on our backs. The articles of clothing inspire the development of new characters and audience suggestions for improvisation.

HOW CHANCE REMARKS TURN INTO PERFORMANCE PIECES

Mildred came to the workshop one day and, with a twinkle in her eye, began to tell the story of her recent pick-up at a bar. Everyone

117

laughed and started to talk about some of the "skeletons" in their closets. From the spontaneous discussion, we got the idea of telling the audience a secret, or something we had never told anyone. Some examples are:

SARA LEE

"This happened many years ago, when my husband, the two children and I stopped at the Petrified Forest. We were traveling home after a trip to Los Angeles. I picked up what I thought was a colored stone and put it in my pocket and forgot about it. Suddenly I realized that this was not a stone, but a piece of petrified wood, and that there was a fine against taking it. So I decided to put it back at the first opportunity.

"The right time never came and before I knew it, we were on our way out of the park. An officer stopped us and asked if the boys took any of the wood. My husband assured the man that they didn't take anything because he watched them very closely. The officer laughed, wished us a pleasant trip, and waved us on. That's the secret I'm sharing with you. Not only was the wood petrified, but so was I. I almost became a jailbird! A thief! You'd never know that to look at me, would you?"

PAUL

Paul tells about his rites of passage from boyhood to manhood. When all his friends visited the local "brothel" as kids, part of the joy of that "first" experience was to tell about it afterward. When everyone was comparing notes, they turned to Paul to get his reactions. He told them all it was *great!* His secret is that he never went in because he was too scared. So, when all the other guys said they had "graduated," he was still in first grade.

MILDRED

"In the Palmer House lobby the other night, I passed a cocktail hour gathering of CPD's (that's certified public drinkers). Now, don't you tell a soul, but one of the sour mashers—age fifty-five and more, I betcha—swooshed and winked my way. Tenderly protecting his cocktail glass from bump-encounter, he invited me to the lounge for sparkling water and conversation to match...me, a pick-up? At my age? At my weight? As Jesus said when he walked on water, *'Anything is possible at any age.'* And that's the secret I'm sharing with you. *Anything* is possible at *any* age."

THE MYTHS OF AGING

These scenes were also inspired by Maggie Kuhn's address. She remarked that she would like to see the day when these myths were proven invalid and never raised again. Through a series of black-out scenes, we have disproved some of the myths in the following humorous fashion.

1. MYTH: Old age is a disease which is irreversible. Old people are physically unfit. SCENE: There is a short scene in which one of the members of the troupe leads the others in exercises (head rolls, leg shakes, arm stretches and jogging). During the jogging, each person makes a lighthearted remark on the sporting life.

2. MYTH: Old age means mindlessness and senility. Intelligence declines. SCENE: Two old friends meet after many years. They discover how busy and involved they are. One is doing volunteer work, studying languages and busy preparing for a foreign tour. The other is going back to school and is a girl-scout leader, off to pick up her hiking boots for the overnite hike.

3. MYTH: Old age is useless. Old people can't do anything of any value. SCENE: This scene shows a vitally active older adult. Her foster grandchildren come to visit, she is baking cookies, she is making arrangements for the club meeting, and is getting ready to go off to her volunteer job.

4. MYTH: Old age is sexless. Old people don't think about or enjoy sex. SCENE: This is a humorous pick-up scene. The woman falls by accident as she passes the man. As he helps to pick her up, they both realize they have met before. He decides to walk along. She ends with the line, "Where should we go?" He answers, "I don't know. Your place or mine?"

5. MYTH: Old age is powerless. Senior citizens have no political power. SCENE: One member of the troupe gets on a soapbox and calls everyone over for a political rally. She decries the *isms* like racism, sexism, and, above all, ageism. She urges the crowd to chant: "WE ISM GOING TO TAKE IT ANY MORE." They go back to their places shouting "Senior power! Senior power!" Here is her speech:
"My fellow voters and taxpayers:

"Aging is not a biological transformation; it is a political transformation! (cheer). Let me introduce myself. I am Raggie Tune. And let me introduce my fellow colleagues: A and B. Welcome to the monthly meeting of the Purple Panthers! We senior citizens look upon aging as a natural process from birth to death. However, we hold that ageism deprives old and young of power and influence. We believe that together we can make our society more just and humane. We demand accountability from government bodies. Let us state our platform. We want:

a. To empower people to control the conditions of their lives—in communities, in nursing homes, in housing developments, in hospitals, in places of work.

b. To change society's attitude toward the elderly, the poor, the handicapped and other oppressed groups.

c. To abolish ageism, racism, and sexism.

d. To develop new life styles that will free us from loneliness and poverty.

e. To enhance awareness of aging as a time of fulfillment rather than degeneration.

f. To create living communities with a diversity of ages, income levels, and background.

g. To end forced retirement and age discrimination in jobs.

h. To build a new power base with other groups struggling for social justice—trade unions, minorities, women—and other liberation movements.

i. To redirect money now poured into military programs to finance national health care, decent public transportation, housing.

j. To change the priorities of society from profits to people.

k. And finally, to grasp our ultimate goal: "SENIOR POWER!" Everyone: "SENIOR POWER! SENIOR POWER! SENIOR POWER!"

6. MYTH: All old people are alike. SCENE: Four people take center stage, one by one, telling the audience their views on "What does retirement mean to me." The four views are quite different and they proceed to argue, culminating in the last lines:

Some are short, some are tall, some are nice,
Some are no good at all,
Summer, winter, spring or fall
We are not alike at all!

The following is a favorite finale of the ACTING UP! players. It has been effective for ending a performance on a positive and energetic note.

It's nice being over sixty-five. My time is my own, my life is my own, and finally, I don't have to wait until I get older to do all those things I want to do. You know why people say life begins at sixty-five? Because when we complain that our arthritis is bothering us, our hair is turning gray—people will say, "Well, that's life!" And I guess it must be. Still sometimes I'd rather be young. But only if I knew all that I do now. Life may not begin at sixty-five, but it certainly doesn't end there. Besides, growing older is something we all do (everyone stands up) EVERY DAY! You lose a tooth. You get a wrinkle. You get married. You have a son. You go to the moon. You work hard. You learn a lot. YOU HAVE THE TIME OF YOUR LIFE—IF YOU KEEP ON ACTING UP!

THE CRITICAL EYE

As a group we discovered that we could really learn what theatre is all about through our group's attending theatre performances in the community. We plan theatre-going parties, after which we discuss the performance. We believe that unconsciously the development of the critical eye will carry over into the players' own performances.

If professional theatre performances are unavailable or not accessible to your group, you might consider high school and college, as well as community theatre performance. Usually there is a senior citizens' discount, group rates, or even free tickets available on certain nights. Don't be afraid to ask; at most you will be refused, but usually the answer is yes! If all else fails, you could go to the local movie theatre together or even watch a television play or movie for critiquing purposes.

The theatre-going experience can be greatly enriched by taking the group backstage after the show to meet the performers. This is especially exciting when the actors are older adults, themselves, and the material of the play speaks to the lives of older people.

We have developed the following form for critiquing theatrical performances, *How to Critique the Theatre Performance,* can be applied to all the forms of theatre described above and can be used in written form or in open discussion. Here is its written format:

121

THEATRE PERFORMANCE

Title of play_____

Date_____

1. Briefly outline the story of the play. Try to boil it down to the central conflict (who is doing what to whom in the play, or, what is actually happening).

2. Which is your favorite character? State why and describe the character.

3. How many major characters are there? Describe them.

4. Did the actors project an "illusion of the first time" in the scene? Was there a feeling of spontaneity and energy?

5. Did the actors reveal the inner character of the roles they were playing? Did you sense a "sub-text," or could you tell things were going on in the scene without words?

6. Were you fully aware of consistent characterization in the scene, or did the individual personality of the actors break through?

7. Was there evidence of total concentration in the scene?

8. What was the overall mood of the play? Do you like the ending? Why or why not?

9. What is the major message of the play?

10. In your opinion, is the play and its performance a good one? Why or why not?

11. If you were the director, what would you do to improve the quality of the show?

12. What audiences would appreciate this show? Why? Is there universality to the play? Can you identify with the play and does it relate to your life as it is today? In other words, does the play have an appeal to a large audience or does it just appeal to a select audience?

TECHNICAL ASPECTS

1. What is the setting? How do you know?

2. How are changes in time and place conveyed? What technical devices are used?

3. How do the make-up, costumes, lighting, set, sound, and props contribute to the overall effect?

4. Was the staging of the scene, including placement of playing areas and entrances, effective?

5. How did the theatre space, itself, affect you? Was it theatre-in-the-round or was it proscenium stage format? Was it a small or large theatre space and was there audience participation?

6. How did you feel when you left the theatre?

AUDIENCE PARTICIPATION

Once you're onstage you have to respond so quickly to a situation that you virtually don't have time to think. There certainly isn't time for inhibitions. You just respond to the situation as you might in real life. The difference is that the situations the audience creates are ones you'd never dream you'd find yourself in.

Audience Participant

Because the ACTING UP! process is a collaborative creation from warm-ups to rehearsed vignettes, audience participation is a natural element of a staged performance. For the members of ACTING UP!, serving as audiences for each other in their workshops is but a small step to involving the audiences who attend their public performances.

Audience participation serves a number of purposes. It takes the pressure of a polished, memorized production off the leader and the performers and builds bridges between viewers and performers. Often an audience is asked for comments, suggestions for improvised scenes, and participation in an actual scene. It is then less likely to be critical about professionalism on stage.

Audience participation generates a strong sense of support between the viewers and actors when they are collaborating on the creation of the performance. It is much easier for the audience to recognize the valuable accomplishment ACTING UP! members have achieved when one is asked to take on the challenge of being on stage as a company member.

Finally, audience participation allows the ACTING UP! members to reach out with comfort and vitality to different age-groups with whom they may not regularly come into contact. We have discovered several "audience warm-up" activities which help to establish the kind of involvement which audience participation will play in the rest of the performance and energize the viewers toward collaboration with the troupe.

Some suggestions for involving the audience are:

1. At the beginning of the show, the leader goes out into the audience and asks various people how old they are and how they feel about

being their particular age. What do you like about being sixty-five years old? What don't you like about it? The leader explains that much of the original material they are performing centers around the ideas of aging and how people feel about it. This sets the tone for the program and elicits humorous responses from the audience. Songs are excellent for involving an audience. A good song to sing with the audience is "No Time At All" from Pippin. Popular "old-ies" are always successful warm-up songs. Consider a sing-along with "Let Me Call You Sweetheart," "It Had to be You," "You're a Grand Old Flag," and "Give My Regards to Broadway" as examples. There may be people in the audience who are either very young or very old. If a person answers that he is in his seventies or eighties, the players applaud him—giving him recognition of his seniority.

2. During the slide presentation some questions can be asked of the members of the audience. Their responses are often lighthearted and add to the comments of the performers.

3. Before going into a sequence on myths, the leader asks the audience for some myths that it has heard regarding older people. A number of myths are explored with the audience.

4. In exercises adaptable to audience participation, such as *The Machine, Add to the Action—A and B, Interviewing the Man on the Street* and *Describe What's Next* (see Stage II), it is easy to include the audience. However, this generally depends upon the nature of the theatre space—how difficult or easy it is to get up to the stage and how inhibited or free the audience is.

5. The audience can be asked to call out the *who, where, what* of a situation and the performers create an improvisation based on the Second City format of improvising a humorous scene in five minutes.

6. We create a *Tug-of-War* with an imaginary rope, dividing the ACTING UP! cast into two sides. Volunteers from the audience are brought up to fill out the short-handed team, after the members of that team complain that they need more help. The rest of the audience is asked to root for the team of its choice. A noisy, active *Tug-of-War* follows with both actors and audience closely involved with the game. (Any sporting event could serve the same purpose of involvement: basketball, tennis, baseball, ping-pong.) Following the "game," an emcee can stage an impromptu interview with the players of the game. We've enjoyed talking with interviewees about ideas such as the oldest player in the major leagues, or how has tennis kept you in shape? Another good one was "I understand you went to China for the international ping-pong tournament. Could

you describe China to us?" Inhibitions drop away at each stage of audience involvement.

7. When the audience is physically warmed up, we ask for two or three more volunteers to create a vocal warm-up. With four members of the ACTING UP! ensemble, these volunteers help to perform the Emotional Symphony. Each performer vocalizes the sounds he or she feels best express the emotions suggested by members of the audience. (See Stage I, *Emotional Symphony.*) After this inevitably funny and uninhibited vignette, we usually discover that audiences of any age are involved and anxious for their next opportunity to collaborate with us.

With an active, interested audience, we often perform a more dramatic and traditional scene, or perhaps, a performance piece which focuses directly on prejudices against older people. We feel the truths expressed in these scenes have more meaning to our audiences at this point. After the scenes we invite the audience to explore with us the message and implications expressed. They have seen for themselves, through active participation, that the actors on stage have an important and personal message worth listening to.

Another example of involving the audience is a vignette that directly focuses on bursting myths of ageism. It was an improvisation called "Dr. Von Stretchmarx and His Amazing Stretching Machine" which has been stylized as an old vaudeville routine. The older actors and audience participate and develop wild and zany characters from history or fantasy who come to Dr. Von Stretchmarx to be cured of the symptoms of various forms of ageism. The actor who played Dr. Von Stretchmarx never knew from performance to performance who might walk into his "office" for a cure by his whacky version of Freud and his stupendous "stretching machine." The cardboard "machine" was a symbol of the transformation process. Audiences of many ages enjoyed volunteering as spontaneous patients suffering from all sorts of "ageism ailments." Both audience and actors learned a great deal through humor and slapstick about the effect of age prejudice on people of all ages.

By involving the audience in the performance the barriers are broken down between the audience and performers. The contact of the audience members with the players on stage makes the players more comfortable and the audience members more vividly experience the process themselves.

POINTS TO REMEMBER

1. Most everyone is a ham at heart. There is nothing that most audience members enjoy more than being asked to help create a

performance. Before asking anyone up on stage, you or a member of the group serving as master or mistress of ceremonies should warm-up the audience by asking questions which elicit evocative, humorous or thoughtful responses.

2. If it takes some time to get volunteers from the audience, watch for audience reaction during a staged piece. Identify those viewers who seem most involved, most open to what is occurring on-stage. Then "select" those people to be involved in a non-threatening group activity like the Tug-of-War. Ask the rest of the audience to be involved and support the volunteers by cheering for the side they wish to win.

3. Even a single volunteer in an entire performance will help you set up a strong connection between audience and performers. Remember that once you've received just one response from the audience, it will be open and ready for more participation. Even those people who do not wish to volunteer to be a part of the performance enjoy watching someone participate from their side of the footlights.

4. Tailor your audience involvement to the specific needs and interests of the viewers. Every audience is different.

5. Treat audience participants as honored guest artists. Escort them on and off stage, and ask for applause for each volunteer after his part in the performance.

Each performance of the ACTING UP! troupe is adjusted to the particular audience. The group performs for elementary school children, junior-high, high school, college, social clubs, senior citizen groups, nursing homes, gerontologists, nurses. Each group has different needs which offer challenges to the leader and players.

Because each audience has its own personality and views the performance in a unique way, it has been helpful to ask the audience members to evaluate the ACTING UP! performance. These evaluations are also helpful if you are considering getting grants from companies or governmental sources. It is often necessary to give an evaluation of your performance. The following is a sample form.

AUDIENCE EVALUATION FORM

1. What part of the show did you enjoy the most?_____

Why?_____
2. What part of the show did you like *least*?_____
Why?_____

_____

3. In what way did the performance change your views or opinions about senior adults?_____

4. Did today's performance make you feel more positive about growing older yourself?_____
Explain._____

5. Have you ever seen another senior performing group?_____
If so, is there anything you saw that ACTING UP! can include in its program?_____

6. What other groups do you know of that might like to see ACTING UP!? Name of group:_____
Contact person_____Phone:_____
Contact Person Only: What kind of feedback did you get from your group?_____
_____
_____
_____

    A large part of the ACTING UP! performance is concerned with bursting some of the dangerous myths of ageism. *The best method for getting your message across, for teaching audiences of all ages that growing old can be an active, vital experience, is by involving the audience in the performance.* Even if the vignettes your group selects to perform do not directly comment on these myths, seeing creative, energetic, mature actors on stage will carry your message to audiences of all ages. And, an audience that has been involved in actively bursting these myths through participation with older actors, is an audience not likely to forget the importance and teachings implicit in that experience.

> We've performed for many senior citizen groups and it may not have occurred to many of them that here is another activity they might participate in. I see all these gray heads out there in the audience and I think it's just possible that these people have felt, 'If they can do it—why can't I? Instead of watching TV, there's another opportunity! I think we might have planted a few seeds in the right direction.
>
> Ben Singer

127

INTERGENERATIONAL ASPECTS

Throughout the years that ACTING UP! has been together, over twenty young student guest artists have collaborated and performed with the group.

> I always knew you could have fun with older people, 'cause my father is a real wing-ding. You just give them a chance and listen to them, instead of thinking you know more than they do.
>
> Karol Kent, Graduate Assistant

> Just because they move a little slower...people think that older people don't know what's going on, that they're not hip to what's going on...These people have lived three times as long as I have and they know!
>
> Michael Chesler, Student Participant

I believe working with the young people has added more fun to our group, on account of their shenanigans. It's made me ACT UP even more. I like it!

Margaret Host

Many of our performances have been for elementary, junior-high, high school and college students. ACTING UP! presents older people who are lively, vital and creative. The older adults' contacts with younger people keep them in touch with how younger people feel, what their concerns and needs are, and how easy it is to bridge that generation gap. It can be a beautiful sharing experience, demonstrating to younger people that being an older person is not the end of life or anything to be feared or disdained. It is shown as another stage of life which has its own rewards and difficulties.

Although the myths of ageism are specific to one age group, all ages have to deal with age discrimination. Young people experience adultism in many ways. They are too young to vote, but old enough to be drafted. Young people are thought to be irresponsible and selfish. They are considered too ignorant about life and the world to make their own decisions. People in mid-life also experience forms of discrimination. They are expected to be conservative, mature, and responsible for everyone. They are not allowed to change once they have established their habit patterns of work, family and friends. Any changes they do make are frowned-upon and considered a mid-life crisis.

Through intergenerational workshops and sessions young and old come up with solutions to their problems. More important, all those involved in the session see that people are not alone and that every age shares characteristic pluses and minuses.

While all the theatre games can be used in intergenerational workshops, we have discovered the most successful activities are based on role-playing techniques. Samples of this type of activity follow the warm-up activities. The former provide a good basis for discussion on those issues the participants wish to deal with, how they feel about becoming someone older or younger, and the problems of these respective relationships.

WARM-UPS AND ROLE-PLAYING FOR INTERGENERATIONAL GROUPS

MIRROR IMAGERY

Match pairs of older people and younger people. One person is the initiator of the movement and the other is the follower. After a time they switch roles where the follower is now the leader and vice versa. The players move in slow motion, looking into each others' eyes. You may call out, "Move face only, hands only, torso only."

AGES OF MAN PORTRAITS

This is similar to the *Emotional Sculpture* tableaux as described in Stage II. Divide the group in half with equal number of older and younger players in each group. Call out the following, as one group at a time forms a group portrait illustrating that age:

1. Babies
2. Nursery school
3. At the circus
4. Coming home with a bad report card
5. First day at junior-high school
6. High school prom
7. First kiss
8. College graduation
9. Wedding
10. First job
11. First baby
12. Physical fitness class
13. First boat trip
14. First mountain climb
15. First home you bought
16. Playing shuffle-board at the senior club
17. Roaring twenties
18. Speakeasy
19. World War II
20. Depression soupline

ROLE-REVERSAL ACTIVITIES

The following are family situations we have presented in our intergenerational workshops with high school and college students. The participants are divided into smaller groups and each group chooses one of the suggestions around which to work a scene. The leader encourages participants to play characters unlike themselves. The older people portray the younger characters and the younger portray the older characters.

1. A young couple is going to live together without being married. They come home to tell the girl's parents.

2. A daughter wants her mother to babysit for her children and the mother has a date.

3. Two retired people want to live together for financial reasons and they are telling their children and grandchildren of their plans.

4. A mother comes upon a surprise visit to her daughter's apartment. The apartment is messy and the girl has several friends sleeping overnight.

5. A grandmother lives in a small house with her chidren and several grandchildren.

6. A young boss calls an older worker into his office to tell him it is time to retire.

7. A young girl confides in her grandmother that her boyfriend has left her.

8. Grandma decides to become a vegetarian and joins a commune. She announces her plans to the family.

9. A family is in the midst of planning a fiftieth anniversary party for their grandparents, as the older adults announce they are in the process of getting a divorce.

10. A father, grandfather and a young son all go out to the local pub. They discover mom, grandmother and girl friend there, having a great time. How do they react?

A discussion should take place after each group performs for the rest of the group. Some possible discussion questions are:

How did you feel about becoming older or younger?

How accurately were the characters portrayed?

Did you learn anything about the kind of person you were playing?

Did you make any discoveries about yourself?

How will this influence your behavior in the future?

A filmmaker once asked us to improvise some scenes around the fears that older people have of younger people and the fears which youth have in communicating with elders. We worked with four younger students at the local community college. The company's response was enthusiastic. Young people who worked with us discovered that their experience with ACTING UP! members was fun. It was an exciting and invigorating exchange of ideas and points of view.

Some of the young people are now part of the company. In one scene two older women sitting on a park bench, see two young fellows "hanging around." They are fearful that they will be robbed or attacked because of what they read in the newspapers, and how the fellows look. The boys are afraid to approach the two older women for fear they will be misunderstood. Finally one of them breaks the ice. After a flurry of concern over their watches and handbags, the boys approach to ask the time. They discover that all four attend classes at a nearby evening school. They wind up leaving together to discuss school and other things they have in common.

Intergenerational to us means coming full circle from youth to age to youth again. Through the theatre games and activities the differing age groups find that they become peers and, better yet, friends.

> I've enjoyed working with the young folks. And I think it proves one point: that no matter what the age, we can enjoy the same things.
>
> Ethel Lanski

> I think that working with the older people has broken stereotypes that I felt about them. They are active and willing to try new things. They are not living in the past. They're just as hip as we are, and really fun to work with.
>
> Jeff Brunk, Student Participant

Through audience participation and intergenerational activities, ACTING UP! reaches out to audiences of all ages: to young people who see and join their elders in performing a program which shares the important thought that growing older is something we all do every day; to people in sheltered care, hospital, or nursing home situations where the image of vital, lively, creative seniors has provided hope amongst the group; to adults with parents who are older adults and who will soon be older adults themselves; to older adults, themselves, who have discovered that "life may not begin at sixty-five, but it certainly doesn't end there!

APPENDIX

Many of the following performance vignettes were developed through group improvisation and threatre games. Please keep in mind that these are "bare bones" dialog notes to the players, and that character expansion and spontaneous fleshing out of the action is an expected part of each new ACTING UP! performance. The short, autobiographical works were written by ACTING UP! members as they exchanged oral histories and worked on formal story-telling techniques.

Not included in the Appendix is the play *Short Stories, Long Lives* written by Marcie Telander and based on oral story telling by ACTING UP! members and seminar participants. This play was written as a structual guide for developing theatre pieces drawn from personal oral histories, written reminiscences and statements about the way life is today. *Short Stories, Long Lives* can be performed as Readers' Theatre or a one-act play, and is available for performance from Marcie Telander, c/o Eyes Productions, 2005 N. Mohawk, Chicago, Illinois 60614, U.S.A.

A CHRISTMAS CAROL FOR SENIORS
by Birdell Provus

(Scene One: Christmas Day in the home of a senior couple, Fred and Marge. A decorated tree stands upstage left, with wrapped presents arranged on floor beneath. Two chairs are in the room, downstage right. Fred and Marge are putting finishing touches to decorating the tree as they await the arrival of their children.)

Marge: D'you know the color I always associate with Christmas?

Fred: Red or green, I suppose. Or maybe white, for snow?

Marge: Nope. It's blue. When I was a little girl, we lived upstairs over a store. *(She stops trimming the tree now and then while she tells the story.)* Our coal-burning stove was in the dining room. There wasn't any stove in the front room where the Christmas tree stood. During the night, the fire was allowed to die down. My brother and I would sneak out of warm beds, shivering in the bitter cold of early morning, to find our present. I can still see that cold, icy-blue light, the first hint of dawn coming through a window thick with frost, touching the tree and the gifts with a pale blue light.

Fred: Uh-huh. *(He pauses in trimming the tree while he tells the story.)* I remember the golden-brown smell of a roasted turkey and the cold, crispy crunch of snow at Christmas time. We always used to gather at my uncle's house for Christmas, everybody driving their tin Lizzies. *(sound of car engines spluttering)* About midnight, when the party broke up, they'd have to wake up sleeping kids, me included, and wade through the snow to the cars. Every year, the men would shove and push and crank to get the cars started. By the time the gang got rolling, it was almost time for the fellows to go to work!

Marge: The tree's so pretty this year. I always say that, don't I? When I was little, during the Great Depression, we all had to pinch pennies. My parents would wait until the last minute on Christmas Eve before they bought a tree. Reduced prices, you know. I was always terrified that there wouldn't be a tree left for us, but there always was. Sometimes we could get one for a quarter or fifty cents. Funny, we're fighting inflation these days, and we're back to pinching pennies.

Fred: Did your folks ever bring a tree home on a streetcar? My dad did, one year. It was a pretty big tree, and the conductor said we'd have to stand on the rear platform. *(sound of trolley bell)* It was cold and crowded, so my dad stuck the tree out over the back railing of the streetcar and held onto the trunk. there were lots of jokes about Santa losing his reindeer, but my father didn't realize that a rag-man and his wagon were plodding along the tracks just behind the streetcar. Apparently the horse was hungry. Very hungry, because when my dad and I got home, he was carrying about two-thirds of a tree! The horse had nibbled a bite at every stop! *(laugh)*

Marge: A likely story! Here, Fred. A very special present from me to you. Open it now so you can be wearing it when the kids come! *(steps to tree and selects gift for him)*

Fred: Aha! One of the well-known gifts for hubby—a Christmas tie, right? *(She leads him to front chair. He opens gift and stares at it.)* Well! My, my! It's *(pause)* very red, isn't it?

Marge: You don't like it! And I made it, I really did, just for you!

Fred: You made it? Of course I like it! It's beautiful! I'll put it on right now. *(He puts on tie, stands up.)* There. How do I look?

Marge: Oh, Fred, you're still so handsome!

Fred: OK, now you've got to open my gift to you. Here, Merry Christmas, dear. *(takes package from table)*

Marge: *(opens gift)* A radio! How wonderful! I'll put it in the kitchen so I can catch the weather reports in the morning. Look how small it is! You know, I'm reminded of the first radio we ever had in my family. My dad gave it to my mother for Christmas. Most of us couldn't imagine what a radio was—this small, magic box with all the voices inside. It was, indeed, a miracle. In fact, it was considered such a miracle I was awakened from sleep and taken out of bed to hear the tinny voices in the marvelous box, the radio. You know, before there were so many stations jamming the air waves, you could get foreign countries sometimes. I remember once my Dad got China! *(She turns on the radio. Immediately, Oriental music is heard.)* Fred! Listen! It's China!

ANNOUNCER'S VOICE: We invite you to bring your family to Hung Woo Chee's Chinese restaurant for your Christmas dinner! *(She snaps off radio and looks at Fred, who laughs.)*

Fred: Not China this time, dear, but I remember listening to the dance bands broadcasting from the Edgewater Beach Hotel.

Marge: Oh, yes! What a thrill that was, such romantic music!

Fred: *(gets up)* Hey-hey! Where's that mistletoe? *(looks up to ceiling)*

Marge: Ah, dearie, we don't need mistletoe for a Christmas kiss. *(gets up)* Come and warm me up this cold winter day. *(They embrace and kiss. She breaks away.)* Well, enough of such mad lovemaking. The children would be shocked if they thought we were still romantic about each other.

Fred: That's right. Old folks are supposed to fade away. How wrong they are. *(moves toward her)*

Marge: *(sounds of arriving car; car door slams)* Oh, oh, is that a car? Yes, the children are here! Come on! *(The two go offstage. Blackout.)*

(Music interval)

(Scene Two: The two are seated in the chairs. Piles of wrapping paper from the gifts are around the tree.)

Marge: Well, they're gone. Time goes so fast when they're here, and all of a sudden, they're gone!

Fred: Now, dear, don't look so sad. We had a wonderful time and we were all glad to see each other. But, you know something? I could use a little peace and quiet. I've forgotten how noisy little ones can be.

Marge: You're right, Fred. It's very relaxing to sit here, just the two of us, enjoying the tree.

Fred: We've shared a lot of Christmases, you and I, but I think this year was one of our best. We're here together, in good health, our children are grown and happy, and we have two wonderful grandchildren.

Marge: I know. We're a lucky pair, aren't we?

Fred: Yup. All we have to worry about now is paying for this year's presents with next year's money.

Marge: We didn't spend as much this year as we used to, and I'm kinda glad we had to cut down. It's not the cost that counts, anyway. It's the loving thoughts.

Fred: That's you, granma. You sure made some lovely things for the little ones.

Marge: We've got a lot of cleaning up to do.

Fred: I've already got some of it done. Last week I cleaned out our checking account and this week I cleaned out the savings account. *(laughs)*

Marge: Oh, Fred! *(pokes him)* I want them to have something to remember us by.

Fred: Yup, I guess that's how we'll live on, in our grandchildren and their memories of us. *(stands up, puts hands in pocket and moves around)*

Marge: *(seated)* I wonder what next Christmas will be like?

Fred: Next year I'm going to give you a present worth fifty dollars.

Marge: *(gets up)* You are? For heaven's sake, what would that be?

Fred: A one hundred dollar bill, what else? By 1982, that's all it will be worth.

Marge: *(with playful slap at Fred)* Don't be pessimistic, dear. We've got each other and that's what counts.

Fred: That's right. You know, Santa Claus is a senior, senior citizen, and he's still going strong. I'm going to give you a twenty-year subscription to Life! And I hope you never run out of Time! *(raises his arm in mock toast gesture)*

Marge: Now, Fred. I want you to be serious for a minute. *(goes to tree and picks up red envelope)* Here's my real present for you, dear. Something I wrote, from my heart. *(comes back to chairs and sits beside him)*

A SENIOR'S CHRISTMAS PAST

Christmases past are a rosy glow
Of childhood memories;
The beautiful doll, the silver skates,
The lovey tinseled trees.

Christmases past include you and me,
And a tiny wreath on the door
Of a tiny flat we were greatful to have
When you returned from the war.

Christmases past recall baby hands,
Reaching to touch a star.
Now the children are grown and moved away;
They keep in touch from afar.

But the joys of Christmas don't end in a day,
Nor come just once a year;
The gift of love, for you from me,
Will never disappear.

Fred: When was the last time I told you I love you?

Marge: My memory's going. Tell me again.

Fred: I do love you and always will. *(He kisses her, then stands and walks to tree.)*

Marge: *(joins him, passing him glass of tomato juice)* Let's drink a toast to the future of the world and to many more merry Christmases! Here we are, toasting with tomato juice! That's about all we can handle these days, but it's just the color for Christmas. Besides, it's got more vitamins and fewer calories than champagne!

Fred: May our future hold as much happiness as our past! *(They click glasses, drink toast, turn to each other and say)* Merry Christmas, Marge!

Marge: Merry Christmas, Fred!

Together: Merry Christmas to all, and to all, a good night!

THE TRIAL

(Characters: Judge, Bailiff, Defense Attorney, Narrator, Defendants, Prosecuting Attorney, Two Confused Women, Woman in Audience)

NARRATOR: A group of Senior Citizens are charged with the crime of growing old. If convicted, they are to be exiled to Florida, where they will be forced to live in retirement villages. They will never see a baby or child again, never see the seasons change, never feel the crips fall air nor see the leaves turn red, yellow and orange. They are to be condemned to play mah-jongh or cards all day long, day after day, and to continuously recite a list of their ailments every hour on the hour.

(Stage Set: The seat provided for the judge should be a high stool, if possible, behind a table or front, representing the judge's bench. An American flag might stand near the facade. Bailiff, defense attorney and prosecuting attorney move around, chat, go over notes, etc. before curtain rises and play begins. Defendants are together. A chair for witnesses is also needed.)

Confused Citizen #1: So what are we supposed to do here? Is it a new TV show or are they making a movie?

Confused Citizen #2: I dunno'. I didn't hear everything they said, but I think we're all going to Florida!

Confused Citizen #1: Oh, great! I wanna sit in the sun and get a tan.

Confused Citizen #2: Listen, at your age, you sit in the sun, you're gonna end up looking like a dried-up prune, all wrinkles and no Oil of Olay.

(Bailiff should "Sssh!" them.)

Confused Citizen #1: I hear they play a lot of cards in Florida. My neighbor goes to Miami Beach and she told me they sit all day on the beach, in the sun, playing cards.

Confused Citizen #2: Oh, cards are all right, but there's another game that's played the beach that's more fun. You place bets on the life-guards, to see which one attracts the most girls.

Confused Citizen #1: Who needs young girls? It's a lonely job, being a life-guard, sitting up there in a high-chair all day. A boy needs some motherly care, a little oil rubbed on his back, someone to fix him a nice sandwich at lunch time, a cold drink, someone to remind him not to go out too far, *(dreamily)* not to swim too soon after eating...

Confused Citizen #2: *(Not interested in her friend's plan for lifeguard care)* Why do the others want to stay here? Brrr, I wouldn't want to go through another Chicago winter if I didn't have to..

Confused Citizen #1: Oh, I think some of them are planning new careers. They look at this trial as a stepping-stone to bigger things. You know, it's getting very popular, to be involved with old people, I mean. I have friends who even rent themselves out for a day or an evening, if the price is right. You know, they'll be the "wise old man," or "sweet little old lady" or any role that's wanted. Professional groups, intellectuals, TV shows, writers, they all want senior citizens now. I'm writing a book, myself.

Confused Citizen #2: Yeah? What is the name of it?

Confused Citizen #1: **How to Be a Salient Senior.**

Confused Citizen #2: What does "salient" mean?

Confused Citizen #1: Outstanding, prominent, striking, important.

Confused Citizen #2: Gee, are you all those things?

Confused Citizen #1: Well, not yet. But I'm only sixty-five. Wait till I'm seventy.

Bailiff: Hear ye! Hear ye! Case of the "Weary Worn-Outs" vs. the "Useful, Youthful, Beautiful Ones." All rise and face the Court. The Honorable Judge Fairman now presiding. *(Faces the audience and motions for entire audience to rise. Defendants rise and stand together, facing the bench)*

Judge: (enters and mounts bench) Well, well! What's this, Bailiff? Another gang bust from the old people's home or were they caught cheating at bingo?

Bailiff: No, your honor...

Judge: All right, let them sit. If they stand too long, their knees may lock, and we've got no locksmiths here.

Bailiff: Be seated, and don't crack your knee joints!

Defense Attorney: Your honor, I protest! The bailiff is ridiculing the defendants.

Judge: Bailiff, no more ad-libbing from you. Any clever remarks made around here will be made only by me! The prosecuting attorney may begin.

Prosecuting Attorney: Your honor, the people before you today are charged with the crime of growing old. They have lost their usefulness. Their parts are either worn out or have been rmoved years ago. They're also slow. Some of them can't see or hear very well and most of all, they're boring, boring, b-o-r-i-n-g!! I intend to show that our society would be vastly improved by removing these old wrecks

Voice from audience: Protest! I protest!

Prosecuting Attorney: *(continues)* from off our streets and out of our homes. Clean up and clear out, I say! We want only youth and beauty around, for their zip and zing and zeal! Let's get going with the go-go's! Let's remove all the old no-no's!

Voice from audience: I protest! You can't do that!

Judge: You paint an interesting picture of the future, young man. Now, let us hear from the defense attorney.

Defense Attorney: Your honor, old wine, old leather, old coins and old friends are treasured throughout the world. Old wine because it is the smoothest, old leather because it is the softest, old coins because they are the rarest, and old friends because they are the truest. I intend to show today that old people are a living treasure, our link with the past. It is not the elderly who are a problem. It is society's treatment of the elderly that is the problem!

Male Defendant: Your honor, I'd like to ask a question.

Judge: Sit down! No one speaks without my permission!

Defense Attorney: Your honor, please alow this man to speak. He has something to say. Hear him out.

Judge: Oh, very well. But keep it short.

Male Defendant:

> Why am I on trial?
> I have some hair left,
> My mustache is not entirely gray
> Yet.
>
> I still ogle the ladies
> I still laugh, giggle and dance...
> Not very well, but I try.
>
> I make up jokes about the elderly.
> In fact, I do all of the things
> That teen-agers do.
> Well, almost...
>
> Of course, I have a few wrinkles
> And my eyesight is not what
> It once was.

But what is there to see
That I have not already seen?
I enjoy thinking about jogging;
That's about as far as I get
But it is a start.

And so, once again, I ask
Why am I on trial?

Judge: Pay attention to the proceedings and you'll soon learn why you're on trial. And I will not tolerate any further interruptions! Call the first of the accused.

Bailiff: Defendant #1. *(Defendant goes to witness chair)* State your name and age, please.

Defendant #1: My name is_____and I am_____years old.

Bailiff: Do you solemnly swear to tell the truth, the whole truth and nothing but the truth, so help you, God?

Defendant # 1: I do.

Bailiff: Be seated.

Prosecuting Attorney: *(may improvise one or two questions here, then asks)* Isn't it true that you are a parasite on the economy?

Defendant #1: Not since my husband died.

Prosecuting Attorney: Oh, you mean your husband provided for you in securities, investments, etc?

Defendant #1: No, sir. My husband left me nothing! Nothing but old bottles to throw out.

Prosecuting Attorney: Then, may I ask, how are you earning your own living?

Defendant #1: Now I get paid for what I used to do for nothing.

Prosecuting Attorney: You don't mean you...

Defendant #1: Yes, sir. I do a good job, too. After I learned how to satisfy my husband, I knew I couild satisfy anybody, so now I do it and get paid for it!

Prosecuting Attorney: Please, madam, exactly what is it that you do?

Defendant #1: Why, I'm the product of thirty-five year training. All those married years, he was always criticizing and demanding, and, as a result, I'm just about perfect.

Prosecuting Attorney: Madam, I ask you, what do you do?

Defendant #1: I'm a professional housekeeper. And I'm supervisor of maid service at one of the large downtown hotels. You see, living with a perfectionist taught me to clean house right from top to bottom. And so that's how I earn my living.

Prosecuting Attorney: Than you. That's all.

Bailiff: Next defendant! *(Defendant #2 takes stand.)* State your name and age, please.

Defendant #2: My name is_____ and I'm_____ years old.

Bailiff: Do you solemnly swear to tell the truth, the whole truth and nothing but the truth, so help you, God?

Defendant #2: I do.

Bailiff: Be seated.

Prosecuting Attorney: You are accused of taking jobs away from young adults with growing families.

Defendant #2: I work for an insurance company, half-rime. And I think your attitude is un-American. President Reagan, our most distinguished senior citizen, has asked that all able-bodied Americans continue working to age seventy-five. And I intend to do just that.

Voice in Audience: Right on!

Bailiff: Defendant may step down. Will the next two defendants please come forward? State your names and ages:

Defendant #3: My name is_____and I'm_____years old.

Defendant #4: My name is_____and I'm_____years old.

Bailiff: Do you both solemnly swear to tell the truth, the whole truth and nothing but the truth, so help you, God?

Defendant #3: I do.

Defendant #4: I do, too!

Prosecuting Attorney: You represent the group of elderly employees. Society accuses you of not measuring up to younger workers.

Defense Attorney: Will the defendants kindly proceed to explode that myth? Evidence, please.

Defendant #3: Not measuring up?

Defendant #4: Do you know who we are?

Defendant #3: Yes, do you know who we are?

Defendants #3 and #4: We are a psychiatrist.

Defendant #4: We are the only shrink who works exclusively with split personality. To speed up the cure, we work with both halves of the brain at once. I do the left-hand side.

Defendant #3: I do the right side.

Voice from Audience: Myth exploded: Bang-bang!

Bailiff: You may be seated. Will the next defendant please take the stand. State your name and age.

Defendant #5: My name is_____and I'm_____years old.

Bailiff: Do you solemnly swear to tell the truth, the whole truth and nothing but the truth, so help you, God?

Defendant #5: I do.

Prosecuting Attorney: Isn't it true that you delayed pacemaker surgery until Medicare could take care of it?

Defense Attorney: Coincidence. Circumstantial evidence! Guilt by association! Let the defendant speak.

Defendant #5: Oh, no, sir. Not true. Luckily I had no need for a pacemaker until some two years ago. You know, that darn thing makes my garage door go up every time a pretty girl goes by!

Judge: *(as witnesses and audience laugh)* Order in the court!

Voice in Audience: That's the spirit!

Bailiff: You may be seated. Will the next defendant take the stand, please? State your name and age.

Defendant #6: My name is_____and I'm_____years old.

Prosecuting Attorney: You are accused of being a doddering idiot. How say you?

Defendant #6: With all due respect, sir, your youth is showing and your manners slipping.

Defense Attorney: *(to defendant)* Ha! You're right to object. Your breeding exceeds that of the prosecuting attorney. Now, speak your truth.

Defendant #6: The number of people over seventy—and over eighty - who are continuing with studies and earning degrees is growing every year. Why, down in Florida, ol' Virge Connor got his Master's degree at eighty-six and, at ninety-two, he's finally made it to Ph.D. We who are standing on trial here—we, too—have learned.

> If nothing more,
> We have learned
> Patience.
> And yes, mercy, too.

> We have learned to survive the stares of youth
> Who notice that

We are growing old, and
Who let us know,
In their superior way,
That we are not long for this world.

But, I say to you, young friends,
You also have but a little way to go
Before you will stand
Where we stand now,
To be judged by those as yet unborn.

Do you now why you are here?
You are here because we brought you
Into this world.

We educated you, and
When you were very young,
We were your first gods.
And now, you would
Banish us from your sight.

(applause from audience)

Voice from audience: Well said, sir! Well said!

Bailiff: You may stand down. Next defendant, please come forward, state your name and age.

Defendant #7: My name is_____and I'm_____years old.

Bailiff: Do you swear to tell the truth, the whole truth and nothing but the truth, so help you, God?

Defendant #7: Eh?

Bailiff: Doyousweartotellthetruth, thewholetruthand nothing but the truth?

Defendant #7: Why, of course! I always tell the truth.

Prosecuting Attorney: The complaint has been lodged that you are hangin' in there too long.

Defendant #7: Eh?

Defense Attorney: He is saying, madam, that you are living too long. Go on, tell it like it is!

Defendant #7: Well, at times I do get winded playing rummy, and sometimes I sit in my rockin' chair and can't make it go, but I'll never stop looking forward to my next birthday!

Voice from Audience: Applause, applause!

Bailiff: Next defendant, please take the stand. State your name and age.

Defendant #8: My name is＿＿＿＿＿and I'm＿＿＿＿＿years old.

Bailiff: Do you swear to tell the truth, the whole truth and nothing but the truth, so help you, God?

Defendant #8: I do.

Prosecuting Attorney: The accusation stands that you and your contemporaries are all hypochondriacs.

Defense Attorney: What do you say in defense to that,＿＿＿＿＿? Is it true?

Defendant #8: Oh, no, sir. Let me tell you about my English cousin, Harry. Is he every healthy! He's 101, you see, and divorcing his sixty-five year-old wife. He feels Jennie just ain't... healthy enough. He says he gave her nine precious years of his life and now at his age, he needs a woman to give him care 'n comfort. You know what I think? I think this divorce is gonna get him in the Guiness Book of Records as England's oldest divorced man. So who says "hypochondriac"? I say "hallelujah!"

Voice in Audience: That's the real spirit! Give 'em the "Old Harry," Harry.

Bailiff: You may be seated. Will the reamining defendants now come forward. State your names and ages. Be seated.

Defendant #9: My name is＿＿＿＿＿and I'm＿＿＿＿＿years old.

Defendant #10: My name is＿＿＿＿＿and I'm＿＿＿＿＿years old.

Defendant #11: My name is＿＿＿＿＿and I'm＿＿＿＿＿years old.

Defendant #12: My name is＿＿＿＿＿and I'm＿＿＿＿＿years old.

Bailiff: Do you swear to tell the truth, the whole truth and nothing but the truth, so help you, God?

Defendants: *(in chorus)* I do.

Prosecuting Attorney: Simply put, society accuses you of aging.

Defense Attorney: Sock it to 'em, ol'timers.

Defendant #9: OK, so sometimes my mind makes contracts my body can't meet.

Defendant #10: So what if I do walk with my head held high, trying to get used to my bifocals?

Defendant #11: I admit, after painting the town red, I have to take a long rest before applying a second coat.

Defendant #12: Sure, sometimes I sink my teeth into a steak and they stay there!

Prosecuting Attorney: Well, madam, what do you have to say for yourself?

Defendant #12: I got plenty to say, buddy! You got no right to put me on trial. I'm earning my own living and what's more, I employ three others.

Prosecuting Attorney: You're an employer? What kind of work do you do?

Defendant #12: I'm the leader of a band, the Rocking Chair Rock Group. We call it the Groovy Grannies. How does that grab you?

Prosecuting Attorney: I've never heard of a senior rock band. How's business?

Defendant #9: It's great! Instead of creating new tunes, we're reviving the oldies, but goodies. Here's a sample. Remember this?

Defendants #'s 9, 10, 11, 12: *(suiting action to the song)*

> First you put your two knees close up tight,
> Then you swing 'em to the left,
> And you swing 'em to the right.
> You step around the floor kinda' nice and light,
> And then you twist around and twist around
> With all your might.
>
> You spread your lovin' arms way out in space,
> Then you do the Eagle rock with style and grace.
> You put your left foot out, then you bring it back,
> That's what we call ball and the jack.

Defendant #10: See, we don't do punk rock. We do the Eagle rock!

Prosecuting Attorney: And for this you get paid?

Defendant #11: Sure! Nostalgia is very big right now, you know. We perform at a lot of antique fairs and children's shows. Those who've never heard it and those who remember it are our biggest fans.

Defendant #9: Like seventy-five year-old...

Defendant #10: Janet Gaynor says...

Defendant #11: Old age isn't so bad...

Defendant #12: We prefer it to the alternative!

Voice from Audience: Right on!

Other Defendants: That's right! You tell 'em, kid! etc.

Judge: *(pounds gavel)* This court will be cleared unless there is absolute quiet! I will not tolerate any further disturbances!

Defense Attorney: Your honor, my apologies for my clients' outbursts. There will be no more, I promise you. Defendants, you may make your final statements.

All defendants: (form a line and speak in chorus)

> Sharing life's enrichment,
> Both past and yet to be,
> The wealth of all we were and are
> We hand you—joyously.

Judge: I am now ready to hear the summation of each attorney. Mr. Prosecutor, will you speak first.

Prosecuting Attorney: *(summation read from notes taken from briefcase)* Ladies and gentlemen of the jury: I'll grant that seniors have better attendance records than their younger contemporaries, and older employees are often more productive. But, I say, not often enough. Let me bring up aging with respect to working. When the aging process begins, around sixty, all processes in the older person's body and mind slow up. This affects their working skills, both minds and hands. I repeat: all physical and mental processes slacken with age. Oldsters may do more work than younger people, but look how long it takes them to do it.

May I also remind you that some of the defendants amitted they don't always get their bodies to do what their minds suggest? Can't make a rocking chair go, can't see too well, can't eat properly? One said he still ogles the ladies. So? All that proves is that he's a normal sexist male. He says he "thinks" about jogging, but doesn't do it. Too many of our elderly do the same thing. They think, but don't do! Today's world calls for doing, not dreaming!

My esteemed colleague, in her opening remarks, said that the elderly are not the problem, but that society's treatment of them is. I disagree emphatically! Look what society does for the elderly! There's low-cost housing, Social Security, SSI, Medicare, Medicaid, counseling centers for the disturbed—all these for seniors! An unappreciative society? I think not! So let these defendants go to Florida and roast their arthritic joints in the hot sun! Let them recite a list of their physical ailments to each other every hour on the hour. They'll tell about 'em anyway, to anyone who'll listen! I rest my case.

Judge: Thank you, Mr/s_____
And now, we'll hear the summation of the Defense Attorney.

Defense Attorney: *(summation read from notes taken from briefcase)* Ladies and gentlemen of the jury:

I couldn't agree more with my worthy colleague, who says, "Let them go to Florida! Let them roast in the sun." Listen, someone should only make the same offer to me. I'd be out of here in a flash. What punishment is this, to be exiled to Florida? What pain is involved in lolling in the sun, walking the beaches, lounging in hotel lobbies? Why, I'd love it! You'd love it! We should all be so lucky!

Ah, but our old folks are not fooled by this Cracker Jack gift from society. Oh, no! Send them to Florida, send them to California, send them to Mexico. It doesn't matter. The heart of the matter is that they are being sent anywhere. They're being exiled! You are trying to get rid of them!

The Eskimos, so legends say, used to put their old folks out in the snow to quietly freeze to death. Well, we've been having very mild winters recently, not enough snow to freeze a turkey, let alone, grandma!

America is fast becoming a throw-away country. Yesterday's architecture is today's parking lot. Cars have been designed with planned obsolescence in mind. Safety razors, pens, paper towels, napkins, plates, handkerchiefs, all are designed to be used once and thrown away. And that's what you are about to do with your old people, throw them away!

Scrap paper drives, scrap metal drives, every neighborhood has a collection spot. But I've never heard of a drive for scrap seniors, have you? Well, there should be a drive for scrap seniors. They've got plenty of usage left in them. And there are many who would bid for their services. The trouble with the prosecution is that it's trying to throw away living history to settle for the capsulated contents of memories through movies. It wants to forget yesterday and replace it with tomorrow.

At the same time, nostalgia is very big in our current society. Doesn't have to be really old to be collectible. Something that dates from the depression of the thirties is desirable today. That means I'm desirable. I date from before the depression. My clients here before you are doubly valuable. They survived the hard times and now they deserve the good times.

Here you are, with living collectibles all around you. Your piece of nostalgia is as near as grandma and what's more, she has stories to tell that have never been recorded. Ask her about them when she comes home from the office tonight!

Judge: I thank you both for your fine presentations. I will ask the jury for its verdict. However, I will render the final decision. This particular jury will tolerate differences of opinion, but I will pronounce the final judgment.

Bailiff: You are now invited to give us your comments on the case that you have just heard. *(Bailiff encourages responses from general audience as to whether defendants guilty of growing old and if punishment should consist of exile or banishment to Florida If not enough audience respons, plants from cast may comment.)*

Voice from Audience: I just wanted to say I have attended trials all over the country and I am shocked, horribly shocked, to find that these innocent people are on trial merely because they're old! And exiling them to Florida? Let me tell you a few things about Florida! You know what bugs me? There are huge cockroaches there, some of which fly! There are large spiders all over, and worse, they have scorpions that hide in your shoes at night and can poison you, too! And, like the song says, "It's too darn hot!" Oh, it's shameful treatment—shameful!

Bailiff: Thank you, madam. Would anyone else like to express an opinion concerning the people you have just seen here on trial? *(calls on any responses)*

Judge: *(after audience response is completed)* Yes, the defendants are guilty of growing older. But, so are we all. None of us can escape, so can it be a crime? Can we call the natural process of living and dying a crime? No. The defendants are graduates of lifetime learning and this is their commencement, a commencement of reaching out for new experiences, deeper understanding and greater knowledge.

So, to society's elders, we award the traditional diplomas representing the closing of one chapter in their lives and the beginning of the new.

Bailiff: Please come forward when I call your name and accept your diploma from the judge.

Judge: Court is adjourned. *(Bailiff calls names, judge distributes the diplomas and shakes the hand of each participant.)*

SENIOR SECRETS
By Birdell Provus

We are all aware that the worship of youth, which handicapped women for so many generations, is now a thing of the past. Fortunately, it has been recognized that the senior citizen is the symbol of success. Only after you have practiced living for sixty or seventy years do you catch on to the secret of surviving. But we have great news for those who still suffer the embarrassment of being young. For all of you under forty, Whistler's Mother, a subsidiary of Age-Old Beauty Corporation of America, is proud to present a new concept in beauty. Something you have all been waiting for—**Senior Secrets!**

Have you always yearned for that lucky day when you find your first gray hair? Are you tired of waiting for Mother Nature to wrinkle your brow, line your face and thin your hair? Do you, too, want to look like an experienced woman of the world? Then **Senior Secrets** is for you. If you're between twelve and thirty-nine years of age, try our products and feel the immediate thrill of instant aging. Within minutes you can have the appearance of a sixty, seventy or even eighty-year-old woman.

We carry the **Dowager Collar** for that definite dowager hump. It comes in assorted colors and sizes, is comfortable to wear, and washes well. We carry **Laugh Lines** for both your cheeks and your eyes— Easily stuck on, can be worn from twelve to fourteen hours and are reusable. We have **Tinted Eye Bags** for that haggard, worn look and something brand new—**Heavy Lashes** to clip to your upper lids. They drag them down and give that "seen too much," sophisticated air so popular with the young set. Individual hairs, *(packaged name of* **Chinny-Chin-Chin**) are meant to be attached to your chin. They are sold five to a package. Pliable plastic **Winkie Wrinkles** are available for the brow, neck, cheeks and hands. **Sequined Liver Spots** are on special this month, three for one dollar and can be worn on either hand. **Double and Triple Dip Chins** are easily attached. They hang from the ears, completely cover the neck and can be worn as mufflers in the cold weather.

When you wear your evening gown, you'll surely want to add our **Flabby Abby Arm Packs.** This flesh-colored, clever disguise is worn under the upper arms, giving a swinging-quivering illusion of lost muscle tone.

Baggy Boobs come in all sizes and are in great demand for that "worn-down and worn-out" look so desired by young women today.

Copyright, © 1980, Birdell Provus

They are available in different lengths, from the **Waist Whoppers** and the **Belly Bumpers** to the **Knee Knockers.** Or, you may want to go all the way with the **Over-the-Shoulder Tossers.** And now, a special announcement for your younger customers: Do you know what varicose veins are? Does your grandma have them? They're lovely blue and purple designs that sometimes appear on the legs of older women. Oh, you can have a tracing like a star or the markings of a river! Or a map of your favorite vacation spot, if you get one of our **Lovely Lines for Limbs,** a special kind of pencil which will allow you to draw your very own varicose veins on your legs, just like grandma's.

Surprise your family tomorrow. Meet your husband at the door wearing our beauty aids. Hear him say those special words: "Ma! Ma, is that really you?" And when the chidren tell him, "That's not Granma, Daddy, that's Mama!" he'll never believe it. Delight your little daughter with the **Sequined Liver Spots** or the **Pliable Plastic Winkle Wrinkles.** What a wonderful gift for a sweet sixteen party.

The above items are carried in all better-class department stores and boutiques, such as K-Mart, Venture, and Walgreen's .

MATURE MAKE-UP FOR MACHO MALES

It's no secret that women, especially younger women, have a preference for older men. Do these names mean anything to you? Cary Grant, Henry Kissinger, Ari Onassis, Ronald Reagan, Frank Sinatra? Why are these older men, these senior citizens, so popular with young women?

The reasons are rather obvious. An older man is more settled in his ways. One can depend on him. He is usually more successful in his chosen field and has already reached the top. Not the least reason for a young lady's preference is the fact that older men are wealthier than their sons, nephews or grandsons. They are also more prone to...heart attacks.

Copyright, © 1980, Birdell Provus

Do the girls pass you up because you're young, with a full head of hair and a lean, muscular body? Cheer up! **Mature Make-Up for Macho Males** has come to your rescue. No longer need you walk around looking like a virile, handsome disco dancer. Get with the new, glamorous grandpa look. Seek out the sensuous seniors' scene. Get in the mode of the moldy millionaires.

Now the truly successful money-maker has probably lost a dozen hairs for every dollar he's made, which leaves him with an empty skull, but a full bank book. Or, his hair may have turned white with the worries of adding up his bank account while he's subtracting his teeth. So our company, MMmm, for short, sells wigs in a wide range of color—gray or white. If there's silver on top, there must be silver down below, right where it counts, in the safety-deposit box!

We also sell hair dye in the same variety of color—gray or white. A third solution to the hair problem is our **Disco Strip** number, which gradually takes it all off as you use the dye, leaving a shiny scalp and a few wisps of hair. This is popular with the boys on Wall Street. Remember, you want to look like a Chairman of the Board, not a champion of the surf board.

Many males today are very health-conscious and do a lot of exercising. However, if you observe carefully, you'll notice that the really wealthy man, the billionaire, hires someone to do his exercising for him. Therefore, his really impressive pot-belly remains visible for all to envy. And how do you acquire in one day a belly that took forty years of gargantuan garbage to build? MMmm puts out a line of belly pads so realistic that you order them according to the amount of wealth you wish to portray. A millionaire size is forty-two inches around the waist. Ten millions comes in a fifty-two inch waistline. Guaranteed to fit.

Men's colognes are very popular today. The sweet smell of success can be yours through our MMmm Company's two popular fragrances, Derrick #1 and Derrick #2. Each carries a recognizable odor of oil wells, #1 from the western state of Oklahoma and #2 from that great state of Texas.

Our products are sold by mail only and are delivered in plain brown wrappers. Check the advertising section of **The Millionaire's Monthly Magazine** for our address.

THE ABSOLUTELY AVERAGE ALL-AMERICAN SENIOR CITIZEN!

by the ACTING UP! Company

(Scene 1: Onstage are Miss Greeley, administrative assistant to Ms. Farshlanger, account executive for a large advertising and public relations agency.)

Miss Greeley: *(visibly upset and worried that things are not going well)*

Ms. Farshlanger: *(enters in a flurry of self-importance)* Well, Greeley, have you found him or her yet? We don't have any more time and there' only one more applicant!

Miss Greeley: No, I just don't understand it. No one seems to fit the profile and I've interviewed so many people.

Ms. Farshlanger: You have been entrusted with a very important duty, to find the **Average American Senior Citizen.** This is a big public relations campaign. A lot of money is riding on this. We've got to sell being over sixty-five!! This is the biggest campaign on old age that anyone has ever done, and if we don't find someone to play the role of our average senior citizen, we might as well kiss the biggest account of our careers good-bye!

Miss Greeley: Yes, Ms. Farshlanger, but no one seems to fit into our stereotype. I mean there don't seem to be any average standard senior citizens around.

Ms. Farshlanger: There is one more applicant outside. I don't know who sent him around, but he looks like the type. He's our last hope, so see if you can't railroad the thing through. Slip a few things by, huh? You know what I mean? His name is uh, Mr. Weinstein, or somethig like that. Now go to it, Greeley! Everything is dependent upon you. Get us, or make us, the **Average All-American Senior Citizen,** or else!

Miss Greeley: *(quite flustered)* Yes, Ms. Farshlanger, I'll try my best.

Ms. Farshlanger: That's not good enough. Do it! *(exit)(Enter Albert Einstein, a gentle, tolerant and humane man.)*

Miss Greeley: Hello, Mr. Weinstein, is it?

Einstein: Einstein, young lady, Albert Einstein.

Miss Greeley: Oh, yes, of course, well, so many of these names sound alike, you know, it's hard to recognize some of them. Forgive me.

Einstein: Don't you worry, young lady. I'm just happy to be of some help. What can I do for you?

Miss Greeley: Mr. Wein—I mean Einstein, we here at Big Time Advertising Productions are auditioning people over sixty-five. You are over sixty-five, aren't you?

Einstein: I've been working for the past sixty years, and I feel as if I'm at the best age yet. Yes, I'm sure I'll fit in there, my dear.

Miss Greeley: Oh, good! We're off to a great start. I can just see you now, Mr. Einstein—we're going to make you famous, make your name a household word. Everyone will remember you. We would like to make you our figurehead for the biggest campaign ever. We're pushing Old Age, you see, and we'd like to audition you for the **Average American Senior Citizen!!!** Wouldn't you like that, being famous for once in your life?

Einstein: That sounds like something I might be able to handle, but just what do you need to know about me.

Miss Greeley: We have a little questionnaire that we would like some answers to—just routine. I'm sure you'll fit right into the stereotype—I mean, the picture—we have imagined for our average senior citizen role.
1. Do you find yourself tired, less physically capable, than when you were before you turned sixty-five?

Einstein: Hmmm, well, you know, just a couple of years ago, I slept only two hours a night. Now I need about three or three and one-half hours.

Miss Greeley: Good, good. *(writes)* Feels he needs more sleep than he used to.
2. Can you sit and play cards for at least eight hours without moving?

Einstein: Card-playing is a nice hobby, but I, myself, can never seem to find that much time to just sit. I play the violin in my spare time. I study very hard at it.

Miss Greeley: Oh, well, you can't win them all. I'm sure we can answer the others correctly.
3. Has your memory been failing you lately?

Einstein: It's interesting that you should ask that, young lady. Just before I came over here, I was writing an equation on the blackboard for some students of mine and some of the people I work with. Actually, the equation took four blackboards, (chuckles) and I noticed that the equation didn't look quite right somehow. You know, I had forgotten a decimal point right in the middle.

Miss Greeley: Wonderful, Mr. Einstein, now we're really getting somewhere—*(writes)* "forgetful." But, you said you have students and you are working with someone. You're over sixty-five, so certainly you must be retired.

Einstein: No, I work on my own, you see. I have a little laboratory at my home and some students, some consultation.

Miss Greeley: Oh, that's better—a hobby! Just some fun equipment down in your basement to putter around with. I see.

Einstein: "Putter." I don't believe I know that word.

Miss Greeley: Oh, don't you worry about that. Leave it to me. Now, 4. Do you watch TV? most of the day?

Einstein: Mein Gott, no! There's so much to do, you see, so much that excites me, so much to finish of my work! Is that required, to watch TV?

Miss Greeley: Well, yes, we had rather hoped so—but let's press on. 5. Do you spend most of your time reminiscing about the past?

Einstein: My dear, there really is no separation between the past and the present for me. My work continues. I have good friends. Why would I want always to live in the past when there is so much for me now—and tomorrow—so much to look forward to!

Miss Greeley: Oh, goodness, it doesn't look too good. Please Mr. Einstein, try to fit into the role, won't you?

Einstein: *(very excited)* No! I have been working to protect mankind and control the making of atomic bombs. Even now I am angry just thinking about it. Oooooooooooh! (He shakes fist.)

Miss Greeley: There, there, Mr. Einstein. Don't worry yourself over these things. It just won't do any good. And right now we have somethig even more important to consider. I have to find the **Average All-American Senior Citizen.** Now, that is important!

Einstein: Of course, my dear. I understand how important all this is to you. I will help you, if I can. Please continue.

Miss Greeley: *(very discouraged, but trying to keep a stiff upper lip)* This is our last chance, Mr. Einstein. It's an open category, so perhaps, we might just be able to squeeze you by, if you have anything—anything—we could use. 7. What experience and accomplishments do you think make you the right choice for our average senior citizen role? Please, Mr. Einstein, I'm counting on you now!

Einstein: Oh, my! Well, I'll surely try. Let's see, I am really rather indebted to Galileo and Newton for my work. Did you know that both of them continued to practice, teach and invent late into their seventies? Oh, dear, I'm off the point. Well, I have a few theories under my belt— I think they've been rather helpful. The theory of relativity is really my greatest accomplishment.

Miss Greeley: Mr. Einstein, you're not trying! Theories aren't experience. Is there anything more?

Einstein: I've been teaching at Princeton for some time—oh, and I have written a number of books. Have you read **The Meaning of Relativity?**

Miss Greeley: *(wailing)* No, I need real experiences. Yours are far too specific. We want *(pause)* generalness, you know, general experiences. I just don't see how we could, well, use your experience in our campaign. We need something really human.

Einstein: Perhaps you are looking for someone older than myself. I have a good friend who is seventeen years older than I. We collaborated on a book together. His name is Sigmund Freud.

Miss Greeley: Thank you, Mr. Einstein. I'm ready to give up. I just can't find anyone to fill the role. Oh, and there's so much to do yet with the campaign and so little space or time.

Einstein: Perhaps I can help you after all. Read my space-time continuum theory. I think it might help you understand and feel more peaceful with the relativity of things. Good-bye, my dear. I enjoyed meeting with you.

Miss Greeley: Thank you, Mr. Einstein. Secretly, I'm glad you didn't fit the role. Somehow I have the feeling that you'll make it without Big Time Advertising Productions. Good luck to you, sir. *(Albert Einstein exits.)*

Ms. Farshlanger: *(enters, rushing)* Well, Greeley, what happened? Didn't you snare him?

Miss Greeley: No, Ms. Farshlanger, and I don't think there is such a thing as an **Average All-American Senior Citizen.** I think it's a hopeless search.

Ms. Farshlanger: Nonsense! We have to make this campaign work. *(She and Miss Greeley rush around setting up four chairs around the table.)* Look here, Greeley. This meeting in a few minutes is our last hope. We're got to get this campaign off the ground.

(Scene Two: Characters are four in-the-field consultants, actors playing themselves; Miss Greeley, the put-upon assistant to Ms. Farshlanger, hot-rod advertising executive. The scene is the meeting room of Big-Time Advertising Productions. Ms. Farschlanger has convened this meeting in order to brainstorm for the biggest campaign of her career, selling old age.

Ms. Farshlanger: *(helps them get seated)* Thank you for joining us, ladies and gentlemen. We here at Big-Time productions need your help in creating the biggest campaign ever for old age, and since you're where it's at, as they say, we're looking to you for some real punch and razzle-dazzle. This is the big one. We've got to sell— sellll—being over sixty-five. It's got to be snazzy, real show biz *(kazoo—to the tune of "Hollywood")*. So let's put our heads together, throw a few things out on the stoop and see if the cat licks it up! Now Greeley, what has the creative department got to show for itself?

Miss Greeley: We were thinking more of something with a humanistic touch. The boys down in "creative" came up with—*(timidly)* "Six- ty-five, come alive." You know, with lots of exclamation points.

Ms. Farshlanger: No, definitely not big enough. It's got to speak to me. It's got to be bold! (kazoo - fanfare)

Miss Greeley: *(timidly)* How about "Get bold, grow old," or Grow old, get bold?"

Ms. Farshlanger: It still doesn't speak to me. It's got to talk! Come on, consultants, why don't you throw out a few ideas, give us the homey touch? We'll run a few up the flag-pole and see if anyone salutes.

Consultant #1: I think of growing older as a time of freedom.

Ms. Farshlanger: Freedom, no. That's passe. Freedom was the big word several years ago for the bicentennial. It's old hat. Give me new stuff.

Consultant #2: Now I'm at a point where I'm finally satisfied with my life. I'm happy now.

Ms. Farshlanger: You can't sell happiness and satisfaction. We've got to sell! Give me cold hard facts. Facts are where the money is!

Miss Greeley: Statistics Department pulled these together for us. There are twenty-four million people over the age of sixty-five today.

Consultant #3: And there are more every day. Over sixty per-cent of the people over sixty years old are reasonably healthy and physically fit enough to do anythng they want to do.

Consultant #4: One out of ten people is over sixty-five. By the year 2000, thirty million Americans will be over sixty-five.

Miss Greeley and Ms. Farshlanger: That's me, that's you, that's us!

Everyone: That's right! *(kazoo - fanfare)*

Ms. Farshlanger: Very convincing! But facts aren't really there— where it's at! I need nitty-gritty. Give me reality. Reality is big these days. Give me something heavy. *(kazoo - dirge)*

Consultant #1: If we don't stop segregating people because of an arbitrary age, America is going to lose one of its most valuable assets!

Consultant #2: Retirement should be a matter of choice, not forcible ejection!

Consultant #3: We need intelligent and far-reaching social and economic changes, if we expect to change the quality of life for older Americans.

Consultant #4: Age doesn't stop creative growth. We over sixty-five are an untapped reservoir of expertise. Use us!

Consultant #1: We deserve quality arts, cultural and recreational programs, not to fill our time, but to fulfill our mental, emotional and spiritual needs!

Consultant #2: We need quiet individual commitment from people of all ages, to destroy ageism of all kinds.

Everyone: *(shouting)* We need action!! action!! action!

Miss Greeley and Ms. Farshlanger: *(overwhelmed)* Well, yes, you do have a point—*(with spirit)* yes, yes, action, action!

Miss Greeley: *(getting excited)* Maybe we could have a banner and uniforms and...

Ms. Farshlanger: *(excited)* and a band, all marching across the streets of America!! *(kazoo - Yankee Doodle) (All of the consultants begin to leave. They realize that they are not really being listened to.)*

Miss Greeley: Look, oh dear, they're leaving...

Ms. Farshlanger: Don't go, this is your finest hour. Look what we're going to do for you, for all of you average senior citizens. We need you! It's really beginning to sound BIG!

Consultant #3: Growing older doesn't need a flashy sales pitch. It just needs good old American Appreciation, a realization that aging can be beautiful and fulfilling.

Consultant #4: Remember, youth is a gift of nature, but old age is a work of art.

(Consultants exit.)

Miss Greeley: (as she walks off-stage with Ms. Farshlanger) Old age is a work of art. I never thought about it that way...

Ms. Farshlanger: Great! That's it. That's what we've been looking for. Can't you see it written on buttons, on T-shirts, airplanes sky-writing all across the land? Old age is a work of art. I like it! *(kazoo - Hallelujah chorus - "Messiah")*

POINT COUNTERPOINT
by Birdell E. Provus

(Cast: 1 - Marilyn, a daughter-in-law; 2 - Sarah, a mother-in-law; 3 - Alice, Marilyn's friend; 4 - Mollie, Sarah's friend)

(Stage Set: Each woman sits by a telephone. The two sets of friends are seated at each end of the stage, left and right. The dialogue must be read in proper sequence.

Marilyn: *(picks up phone and dials)* Alice, this is Marilyn. I've just got to talk to somebody. It's all settled. Sarah's coming to live with us.

Sarah: *(picks up phone and dials)* Molly, this is Sarah. I've just got to talk to somebody. My son says it's all settled. I'm to live with him and his wife.

Alice: Your mother-in-law is moving in with you? My lord, where are you gonna put her?

Mollie: You're moving in with your son and daughter-in-law? Oh, you poor thing! Where are you gonna sleep?

Marilyn: Well, we'll have to move the girls together, that's all. Barbara's room can take another bed. Poor kid, she was so happy when we moved here, 'cause she'd have a room of her own, and now she's got to give it up.

Sarah: Well, they're going to move the chidren together. They're young. They won't mind. We slept three in one bed when I was a girl. The kids can lay in bed and talk together after the lights are out. We used to do that.

Alice: Well, I'll miss seeing you at the club and on our shopping sprees. I don't suppose you'll be able to gad around with the old lady in the house.

Mollie: Oh, Sarah, I'll miss you! We won't have our afternoons in the part or be able to go window shopping together.

Marilyn: I suppose not. But she really belongs here, with her family, where I can keep an eye on her.

Sarah: I guess not. But I love my son and my grandchildren very much and it'll be good to be able to keep an eye on them.

Copyright, © 1980

Alice: When is she coming?
Mollie: When are you going?

Marilyn: Next Monday.
Sarah: Next Monday.

Alice: Well, let's get together for lunch tomorrow and I'll commiserate with you.
Mollie: Well, let's meet in the park tomorrow to say good-bye.

Marilyn: OK, Alice. I'll pick you up about 11:30. 'Bye.
Sarah: OK, Mollie. I'll walk over about 11:30. B'bye, dear. Don't worry, it'll be alright.
(The four women hang up the phones simultaneously and leave the stage.)

(Two weeks later. The four women return to their telephones, same as previous scene.)
Marilyn: *(Answers phone after ring)* Hello?
Sarah: Hello?

Alice: Hi, Marilyn, it's Alice. Listen, what's happened to you? Two weeks I've been out of town and I just got back today. I'm dying to know how you're getting along with your mother-in-law?
Mollie: Sarah, darling, it's me, Mollie. For two weeks I haven't heard a word from you! I thought you were dead already! So I looked up your son's name in the phone book and now I'm asking, how are you getting along with your daughter-in-law?

Marilyn: Oh, I dunno. She means well, I guess, but she...
Sarah: Oh, I dunno. She means well, I guess, but she...

Alice: Listen, can you talk now? Is she around?
Mollie: Listen, can you talk now? Is she around?

Marilyn: No, she's on the other phone, talking to a friend.
Sarah: No, she's on the other phone, talking to a friend..

Alice: So what's it like, three generations in one house?
Mollie: So what's it like, one big, happy family?

161

Marilyn: Well, it's not one big, happy family, I can tell you. She's always interfering between me and the kids.

Sarah: Well, not exactly. I can't stand the way she handles the children. If they were my kids, I'd do it differently, believe me!

Alice: Sure, that'd bug me, too. But you know she adores the girls and that's one way of showing her love and concern. Maybe there's more than one way to handle a situation.

Mollie: Sure, but don't forget they're **not** your kids. Would you have let someone tell **you** how to take care of your own kids?

Marilyn: I suppose you're right. I remember my mother used to complain because my aunt didn't approve of the way she reared my brothers and me.

Sarah: I suppose you're right. I remember my sister used to drive me crazy! She never had any kids and yet she always criticized what I did with mine.

(Note: The playlet, at this point, can be turned over to the audience for its suggestions as to how the problem might be solved. A general discussion might follow, depending, of course, on the audience interest.)

Alice: Just remember what's really being expressed by her criticisms, a loving concern for the girls. After all, she did a pretty good job on her son, didn't she? You chose him for your husband and the father of your kids. Right?

Mollie: Just remember, Sarah dear, Marilyn's a young girl. In time she'll learn and maybe the kids will turn out alright, anyway. After all, both the girls look like your side of the family, so how could they go wrong? Am I right?

Marilyn: Right, Alice. I guess I shouldn't get so uptight about it. Richard always agrees with me, whatever I do with the kids. and she loves the girls and they love her and that's important.

Sarah: Right, Mollie. I guess I can learn to keep my mouth shut. After all, they're my son's children, too, and he and Marilyn seem to agree on what they're doing. So, times are different. Well, I love the little girls and they love me and that's the important thing.

Alice: I'm glad you can see her point of view, Marilyn. It'll make things easier for you when she criticizes you. Maybe if you can agree on even a few things about the kids, it'll help, too.

Mollie: I'm glad you see that, Sarah. It'll make it esier for you to remember to keep your mouth shut and don't interfere with the mama and papa and the little ones.

Marilyn: I'll try, Alice. Anything for peace, but it's hard to remember.

Sarah: I'll try my best, Mollie. I want it should be be peace in the house. But it's hard to remember.

Alice: Listen, kiddo! Someday you're going to be old, too. So look ahead and remember she's feeling like an unwanted guest in your house. You're still the "lady-of-the-house," you know. You can afford to be understanding.

Mollie: Listen, dear, you were young once. You remember how you wanted no one to interfere with your life. So look back and remember she's the mistress of your son's house, not you, dear friend. You had your turn. Now it's her time.

Marilyn: Well, I'll try my best. You know, sometimes it's kinda nice to have her here. We even share a joke once in a while. Well, thanks for calling, old friend. I'll see you soon. G'bye.

Sarah: Well, I'll try my best. You know, sometimes it's kinda nice to be here. We even make jokes once in a while. Well, thanks for calling, old friend. I'll ask. Maybe Marilyn will drive me to the bus stop. We'll see each other soon. G'bye.

THE HOWARD STREET EL
by the ACTING UP! Players

(Characters: A young mother; Billy, a four-year-old boy; priest; shopping trip lady; lady of the evening; expectant mother, due any minute; suburban snob; college student; Howie, the hi-jacker; salesman; activist; policewoman)

(Scene: An elevated El train (Howard B.) The train has stopped unexpectedly between stations. The conductor mumbles an announcement on the loudspeaker, but no one can understand what he has said. The passengers who do not know each other start asking each other what he has said and the action begins.)

Everyone: *(talking at the same time)* What's happened? Why are we stopping? Is there an accident? What did he say? I can never hear the motormen. Oh, this is exciting. It happens at least once a week. Not again. I'm in a hurry. *(Gradually, people start talking to each other.)*

Billy: *(pulling at Mommy)* Mommy! Mommy! Why did we stop? Tell them to start. You told me I'd be home in time for Popeye. You lied. Tell them to start.

Mommy: Everything will be OK. The train will start in a few minutes. You'll see. *(digs into purse)* Here's a coloring book and crayons to play with.

Billy: I don't want to color. I want to go home. You promised me an ice cream cone and I want it now.

Mommy: *(nervously, trying to appease)* Now be a good boy, Billy. Here, here's a life saver. That will taste good.

College Student: Gee, I wonder how long we'll be stuck. I'm on spring vacation from school and Freddy, he's my boyfriend, he's meeting me at Howard Street.

Lady of the Evening: Oh, really, honey. I'm meeting a very fine gentleman at Howard Street, too. Let's see, his name is *(She looks at paper she has taken from her purse.)* John Smith.

Student: Oh, that's a nice name. Have you known him long?

Lady of the Evening: Oh, I haven't met him yet, dearie.

Student: Oh.

Expectant Mother: I'm on my way home from the doctor. I feel like I'm going to have this baby any minute, but he says it's going to be at least two more weeks. *(pause...)* Oh, ohhhhh *(hand on belly)*. Is he ever wrong!

Priest: Just be calm, my dear. It's just one pain. It doesn't necessarily mean anything. Try to relax. Concentrate on something else. Have you picked a name?

Expectant Mother: *(still holding stomach)* Well, I like Jeremy, but my husband likes Joshua, so I hope it's a Jennifer. Ohhhh, Ohhhhhh, there it is again. Do you have a watch? What time is it now?

Priest: *(shows watch)* Let's wait and see what happens and not get excited. I'll be sitting right here. Don't worry.

Shopper: I've been shopping all day. Me feet are killing me and now this has to happen. Everything happens to me. I thought it was going to be a nice day and look how it's turning out. With my luck I'll have to return everything, anyway. Better I shouldn't have gone downtown today, but no, Harry had to have his new suit picked up to wear to the Bar Mitzvah tomorrow.

Snob: *(looks up from book she is reading and gives look of disdain)*

Shopper: He was downtown yesterday, but could he walk two blocks out of his way? No, I had to make a special trip downtown on a Friday, of all the busy days, to pick up his suit. Isn't that just like a man!

Snob: *(gives another look of disdain)* And I had to miss the Northwestern and be subject to inner city transportation. Hmph.

Howie: *(a high-jacker, enters from rear of train)* Alright, nobody get excited. Everyone stay in your seats. *(moves up the aisle and sits in a side-seat in front of the snob and the shopper, is obviously nervous and has his hand in his pocket holding a "gun")*

Snob: What do you mean, stopping this train? Are you the cause of our delay? I demand an explanation!

Student: He has a gun!

Everyone: Oh, no! A gun!

Billy: Mommy, I'm afraid. Is he a...a..?

Mommy: High-jacker!

Everyone: A high-jacker!

Salesman: Look, buddy, we don't want any trouble. What do you want? Why do you want to high-jack the Howard St. El?

Howie: For the very reason you just mentioned.

Saleman: What reason? I don't understand.

Howie: The Howard St. El! I'm sick and tired of this train always having to go exactly where it's expected to. Every year, every day, why should it always go to Howard St? Why can't it go to Kedzie and Lawrence, or anywhere else than where it's expected to go?

Snob: But what are you going to do? I can't see what point you can possibly make by stopping the trains. Are you going to hold us for ransom? I've read about these desperate characters. You're all a certain type—shifty, non-conformists, unemployed...

Everyone: Shhh...don't get him upset. He's got a gun!

Howie: *(wheels around and points "gun" at the shopper and the snob)* I just want this train to go to...Kedzie and Lawrence, for once, just once.

Everyone: But why?

Howie: Because they have great Reuben sandwiches at a little place on the corner there. And that's what I want! A Reuben sandwich...

Shopper: I know that place. It's Hy's Deli. Their Reubens are OK, but have you tried their matzoh-ball soup? Mmmmmm. Now if you really want a good Reuben...

Snob and others: *(cut her off, as they don't want to upset him)*

Howie: Everyone stay calm and nothing will happen. I guess it's an electrical failure...

Lady of the evening: Hey, fella, this is all real interesting, but it's going to be New Year's Eve in just a few hours and I've got this very special date lined up. Know what I mean? We all want to go home.

Howie: It's New Year's!! You see, I've already started my New Year, and I made this resolution, a promise to myself. I've lived sixty-five years doing it their way. Now it's time to do it, just once, my way! Can't you understand?

Everyone: *(thinking over this comment)*

Expectant Mother: *(moans)*

Howie: *(gets up from seat and moves behind her, truly concerned)* Try the La Maze method, natural childbirth. Breathe like this. *(They puff together.)*

Expectant Mother: *(between moans)* Do you have children?

Howie: *(proudly)* Four of them! *(sadly)* But none of them live in Chicago.

Expectant Mother: And here you are, high-jacking a train. You should be ashamed of yourself! If I have to have this baby on an El, the least you can do is get rid of that gun. Now give it to me. Come on, hand it to me.

Howie: *(sheepishly pulls a gold pen out of his pocket)*

Everyone: It's only a pen! Why, of all the nerve!

Salesman: *(leans over and takes the pen, holds it up and reads engraving)* "To Howie Baum, happy retirement."

Howie: *(while everyone grows silent)* I've never had a gun in my life. I wouldn't hurt anyone, but today was, well, it was one of the worst days of my life.

Expectant Mother: Why, Howie, what happened?

Howie: Well, every New Years, my factory has a big employee party in the afternoon before New Year's eve, and today, at the party, they told me they were...pensioning me off. I'm sixty-five. I've given them forty good years as a tool and die-maker, and they give me a gold pen.

Snob: Howie, I'm really sorry for my comments. I didn't know, but I still don't understand why you would want to high-jack a train.

Howie: *(beginning to get angry, determined)* We're all on someone else's time schedule, everyone of us, just like this train, going exactly where they want us to go. So just once in me life I wanted to do the...the unexpected. Maybe they can pension me off, but I can still stand up and be an individual. I'm free now. I can do what I want, and right now, what I wanted to do was to get a Reuben sandwich. And, for once, take the Howard St. El to any place other than Howard St.!

Everyone: Alright, Howie! Atta boy, you show 'em!

Shopper: I'm making a brisket for New Year's dinner for Harry and me, nothing special, but the kids are coming over, so I'm making a brisket.

Howie: Oh, I love brisket!

Snob: What is a brisket, some kind of fish?

Shopper: No, it's meat. You put it in a pot and you cook it. It's delicious.

Snob: Mmmmm, and what kind of wine would you serve with that? I think, perhaps a cabernet sauvignon. What is your opinion, Howie?

Howie: I like it with a good red wine. Delicious!

Snob: What do you serve with your brisket?

Shopper: I like Mogen David. It goes good with everything.

Snob: And who is your supplier?

Shopper: I get it at Walgreens, on sale.

Salesman: Oh, I don't mind this at all. I'm too late to catch my plane home tonight, but Howie, thanks. You've given me an excuse to stay in Chicago, and if she's willing, to spend New Year's eve with a very special lady.

Activist: Howie, you're just the right man for my organization. You've got guts, you're an activist! I've been wasting my breath here, but I'm sure you'll want to know all about how the world has been mistreating pigeons.

Voice of Policewoman: This is Policewoman Markoski speaking. We know the high-jacker is in there, and we have spoken with the authorities. They have refused your demand to reroute the Howard St. El to Kedzie and Lawrence! Come out peacefully with your hands over your head and nothing will happen! I will give you exactly thirty seconds to come out!

Everyone: (conferring) What are we going to do? We can't let Howie go to jail!

Howie: It's alright. I'll go. It doesn't matter, anyway.

Everyone: No, Howie, we won't let you do it!

Snob: (to policewoman out window) Officer, what is going on out there? This is New Year's eve and we all want to be allowed to leave the train and go home. Is this some silly CTA scandal the city is trying to cover up? We demand to be released, instantly!

Everyone: (yelling out the window) There's no high-jacker. Let us go home. This is just a mix—up.

Policewoman: No high-jacker? But they said down at head-quarters that... Alright, everyone out of the train, but no funny stuff!

Activist: Listen, everyone, I have a plan. I can hide Howie behind my sign and sneak him off the train. You all go first and get their attention. Then we'll follow you.

Everyone: Great idea. Good!

Howie: (overcome) Wait, before you leave. Thank you, everyone. I...I can't tell you how good you've made me feel. I'm a new man!

Salesman: Attaboy, Howie, keep at it and you'll be one of the most independent individuals going!

Howie: (choked up) I just want to...to...to wish you a Happy New Year!

Everyone: Happy New Year, Howie! Cheers!

Billy and Mommy: (calling to Howie as they leave) Don't forget, Howie, lamb chops at our house!

Student: Bye, Howie, I can't wait for you to meet my friend.

Lady of the evening: That dinner at the little Italian place is still on, right, Howie?

Expectant Mother: (Estelle helps her off the train.) I'm going to name the baby after you, Howie. Hang in there, baby!

Snob: Don't forget, Howie, for your next ethnic dinner, brisket and Mogen David.

Shopper: You can get it at Walgreens on sale! Come and meet Harry and the kids. They'll love you!

Salesman: Thanks again, Howie, for making me late, but this time I'm not too late to renew an old friendship.

Activist: Are you ready, Howie? There's no better time than the present to get the New Year underway.

Howie: *(taking both of their arms)* Well, then, ladies, let's give 'em hell!

(They exit, gleefully singing and shouting "Hooray! For he's a jolly good fellow", etc. and finally, "Happy New Year!!")

Truefriend
by Mildred Bedows

I have a bittersweet remembrance of something that happened that winter of misery in '32. The boarder in our attic was Lathroppe-the-Author. Middle age, I guessed he was, age 23 to my 11. We became Truefriends, Lathroppe and I, and the treasure at the end of my climb to the attic was our sharing of dreams and expectations. Unless he was busy authoring. Then, or course, I would be cat-still, quietly alternating between reading a book and reading Lathroppe's wallpaper.

I loved reading that wallpaper. It was special, so different from anybody else's in my world. Custom designed, you might say, with letters from the editor of **Boy's Life** magazine, **True Confession, American Druggist** and more. All thanking my Lathroppe for sending manuscripts that, regrettably, couldn't be used at the time..."but do keep writing, dear sir..."

Well, of course he kept on writing. And one joyous day the mailman brought a letter from a very smart editor who knew what I had known all along - - - that Truefriend was a genius, a WRITER. "Dear Mr. Ginsberg," read the letter, "we are happy to publish your article, titled **Magic Tricks.** Ten dollar ($10.00) check is enclosed."

I still remember how I nearly burst with delight when Lathroppe, my Truefriend, gave me the letter to read myself; to share with him, his triumph. At last the world has come to recognize his worth, sang the heart.

But the world didn't recognize soon enough. Nor often enough. For one bleak day, battered suitcase in hand, Lathroppe came to us in defeat and said, "There are no jobs in these black times. And the sale of a story now and then is not enough to pay the rent. You are good people, and kind," he sighed, gently stroking my hair in farewell, "and I will remember you always. My depths have been plumbed and so it's goodbye. I have no choice but to return to the family plumbing business in Philadelphia..."

Oh, Lathroppe, Lathroppe, time now tolls your years as 72. But to the remembering heart, you will always be dear Truefriend-in-the-attic.

AUTHORS' BIOGRAPHIES

Marcie Telander, M.A., is a professional writer, performance artist and arts educator. She has conducted workshops in Creative Drama and Writing for elders around the country. Marcie is the author of several plays for senior adults. At present she is implementing interdisciplinary arts programs for young people on grants from the Illinois Arts Council, Colorado Arts Council and the Chicago Council on Fine Arts. She co-directed with Mark Schwiesow the film, *ACTING UP!*

Karol Verson holds a Master's Degree in performing arts from Northeastern Illinois University. Karol is an instructor of Speech and Theatre at Oakton Community College. She has performed professionally throughout the Chicago area. For many years Karol was affiliated with Imagination Theatre, Inc., an improvisational performance company for and with children. Currently she directs the ACTING UP! troupe and Oakton Community College's touring company, The Unincorporated, Truly-Inspired, Way-out Imagination Theatrical Company.

Flora Quinlan, B.F.A., studied acting and directing at the Goodman School of Drama in Chicago. She teaches creative movement and theatre on the junior/senior high school level and directs Children's Theatre classes through local community centers. Flora writes for children and senior adults, and has performed around Illinois as a theatre artist with Urban Gateways. She conducts theatre workshops for directors of elder-care programs and is currently working as a free lance Public Relations Consultant.

BIOGRAPHIES OF THE ACTING UP! TROUPE

Fred Abbott

Fred has sampled many careers. He began by serving in the armed forces in World War II. He has been a guitarist-singer in underground cafes. While semi-retired, he works as an ice cream vendor. Although he travels the longest distance, he comes to the group weekly, but then, he's always been willing to travel for what he wants. He has a natural rapport with audiences of all ages—whether children or senior adults. He has become a polished TV performer in ACTING UP! features and in documentary films. He loves to tell others, in a humorous way, all the things it took him so long to learn.

I was surprised to find out how many members of the group were creative in writing poems and sketches. I'm semi-retired. I work a couple of months in the summertime. I need to because I don't have enough money with social security. I would work anyway, because everyday I make hundreds of children happy. I'm Uncle Red, the Good Humor man. For me, it's important as I grow older to continue to make new acquaintances, meet new people. ACTING UP! has given me a wonderful opportunity to do so.

Mildred Bedows

Mildred is a natural teacher with a keen and inquiring mind. During World War II she worked in the War Department Finance Office, retiring to raise family and flowers. Recently she has become a prolific writer of poetry and fiction and has discovered a new career as a teacher of English as a second language. She is well-versed in literature and is known for her original punning and coining of a phrase.

Originally, creative drive was the focal point in bringing together a group of strangers to form ACTING UP! Its members are of varying socio- economic and ethnic backgrounds, so participation in the group has afforded me a unique kind of personal enrichment. We relate to each other and to all sorts of audiences, hopefully generating tolerance and understanding. I'm proud to be a part of it.

Tom Burns

Tom is a retired teacher and high school administrator/counselor with a zest for life. In his retirement, he has experimented with many new endeavors, including selling real estate, teaching memory courses and teaching lip-reading to the hard-of-hearing. He starred in the Oakton College production of *Moonchildren* and remarked that it felt just like home. He is the father of six children. We hear that he spends a lot of time in "pursuit of the little round white ball." Golf is his sport; he is not yet ready for shuffleboard!

I retired at sixty and became involved in the activities at the Skokie Senior Center and subsequently with the ACTING UP! group. My involvement in this group has given me a realistic and comprehensive outlook on the problems and lifestyle of people who are sixty-plus years young.

173

Flo Echales

Flo is a devoted housewife and mother with an active body and mind. Her sense of humor and European flavor add the spice to ACTING UP! Her natural abilities as a storyteller have encouraged others to tell their stories.

Since joining ACTING UP! I am not bashful to speak in another's presence. I would never open my mouth if there were strangers in the room. Now when I have to, I'll do anything. After my children and grandchildren saw me perform in ACTING UP! they said, 'Mom, Grandma, we didn't know you could do that!' And I said, 'Get to know me, you might be surprised.'

Dorothy Finkel

Dorothy came to ACTING UP! as a recent widow looking for a meaningful activity. She has become one of our natural comediennes. She credits to ACTING UP! her confidence in expressing herself both on stage and in writing.

The moment that stands out was when I read something we were told to write in five minutes. And as quickly as you can imagine, the thoughts came to me. I was shocked when I got through how much I had written and how much I had told about myself. The thing that touched me the most was when Karol gave me a big kiss. She said, "Because it's right from your heart." For a long time I had kept the fact that I lived in an orphanage a secret. And then I thought, 'Why am I doing that to myself?' From that time on I had a different frame of mind.

Paul Giardini

Paul is a retired industrial engineer for Revere Copper and Brass. He has been a member of the Northwest Symphony orchestra and the President of Maine Township Republican organization. He has recently developed a talent for creative writing and he is still active in local politics. Like a typical college student, he has chosen to go to work for the summer so that he can continue to perform with ACTING UP! during the fall and spring seasons.

ACTING UP! has been just great for me. It provides me with an outlet to act crazy and to be someone other than myself. ACTING UP! is a part of a new beginning for me and I keep wondering if it's true that the whole world is a stage and we, you and I, are merely the players.

Bill Grousky

Bill is retired from work at Teletype Corporation, but not from the single life. He is an active square dancer, swimmer and ladies' man. His elegant poetry and fiction have taught us what a writer is: an ordinary man with extraordinary perceptions.

I'm as tall as the average fence post, as wide as two. Hair grey, what there is of it. Shy, retiring, with a good memory of things past, but can't remember a line I heard two minutes ago. I think that I'm easy to get along with. But of course, I am not what I think I am—and I am not what you think I am. I am what I think that YOU think I am.

Margaret Host

Margaret is devoted to family and husband and the good life. She has played organ and piano for many years. She is a composer whose music and lyrics have been published. Since joining ACTING UP! she has become a community organization and social activity leader.

I had a nervous breakdown and I was in that *Emotional Symphony*. I had been more or less taught not to lose my temper. I was supposed to be angry for the *Emotional Symphony*. I got worked up and it frightened me. After that I thought I'd better quit, but I did go back. I found that ACTING UP! was an outlet for things that I couldn't let out. I realized it doesn't hurt to let it out. This was a positive way of getting rid of the anger without really getting upset.

Estelle Jeral

Estelle has been involved in the business world as a bookkeeper most of her life. Her skills in organization helped ACTING UP! to establish itself as a touring company. Recently she has returned to work part-time and has performed in other college theatre productions. She has been an excellent spokesperson for ACTING UP!

One time we performed for a group of gerontologists. They were so delighted with us that they gave us our first standing ovation. It was thrilling to think that we started out as a little discussion group and we grew just like Topsy. Here we were in front of professionals. To me it meant that our efforts and time were all well repaid. ACTING UP! gives me self-worth and a feeling that I am doing something well, I can make somebody laugh. It does things for me.

Maury Krasner

Maury joined ACTING UP! after being forced into mandatory retirement from his career as a tool and die maker. His athletic performance pieces became an important part of the ACTING UP! style and his lyrical poetry has been published in various literary magazines. Maury now divides his time between professional modeling and acting in TV commercials, business consulting, inventing and poetry workshop instruction at Chicago-area nursing homes.

I didn't feel I was as old as everybody else. I am that old, but I'm not that old. For people like me, being a young spirit in an old body, ACTING UP! is the first time in my life I'm stepping out of my role, the role the world sees me in, and I'm projecting thoughts I've always wanted to share.

Ethel Lanski

Ethel may be small in stature, but she is large in talent, leadership and energy. Retired after twenty-three years as a hospital secretary and keeper of birth certificates, she plunged into performing with gusto. She has been interviewed on radio and TV as a spokesperson for ACTING UP!. She travels extensively when ACTING UP! isn't performing and is proud of her large family.

The group has given me confidence in myself. I have discovered I can do things I never realized I would be able to do. By doing these things I am not only giving a little happiness to others but have brought a feeling of a job well done to myself. This has helped me feel that although I am older, life can still be worthwhile. A few of the things that ACTING UP! has made me believe in are:

1. Never say you can't do something until you try.
2. By bringing a little happiness to others, you are making your life worthwhile.
3. Because you are older, you don't have to feel silly or ridiculous doing things you enjoy and want to do.

Inez Mueller

Inez is a multi-faceted person. She has a science degree which has led her to become a student and lecturer in holistic health. She is a published writer of fiction and one of the first participants in the nation-wide elder hostel educational programs. She has never stopped learning or taking classes.

All my life I've believed in the possibilities of stretching my mind, my imagination, my physical body. ACTING UP! furnished an important challenge at a time in my early widowhood when I needed stimulus and companionship. Presently, I am writing legislators concerning the growing dangers confronting our environment, our survival, and our rights as women (ERA) and as individuals.

Birdell Provus

Birdell has led many different lives. She began her first career as a WAVE and moved on to volunteer for PTA, Girl Scouts and the homeowners' association. She then pursued a career as the assistant to the director of personnel at Evanston Township High School. When she retired she decided to fulfill all of her secret desires. She now swims every week, is becoming proficient in French and is taking on a new challenge—the violin. Since joining ACTING UP! she has become a prolific writer and has been published in journals.

I've been very active all my life, but if I were to walk into a crowded room and see no one that I knew, I'd stand in the corner. I never approached people because there was always the fear of rejection. Since I have been in ACTING UP!, I have a self-confidence I never had before. I enjoy entering a crowded room, picking out someone and saying 'Hi.' Taking part in ACTING UP! has given me a sense of freedom to be a new me, a person I have only just met. Can you imagine what it's like to discover a new world after you were sure your own familiar routine was dragging to a halt? To take a walk along a new path that you had never seen before? And, to do and learn new activities when you thought you'd already done it all? I'm flying. At age sixty-six!

Sara Lee Roitman

Sara Lee wandered into ACTING UP! never suspecting what would be in store for her. As a recent widow she was working with her son in the printing business, but decided she needed something of her own. Even though she said she was "shy," she transformed, upon joining ACTING UP!, from a "shy violet into a rambling rose." She is most comfortable in front of a large audience. Her new husband is proud of the fact that she has led workshops for ACTING UP! at conventions and colleges as well as being our costume mistress par excellence.

I've been a widow for some months and I've had a hard time feeling confident. But now, after ACTING UP! nothing is ever going to be the same. I'm not my old shy self any more. With my smile everyone calls me Sara Lee Cheesecake and the pun is intended!

Mary Kerr Smith

Mary K. has braved all kinds of weather to join ACTING UP! from her home in Chicago, traveling on public transportation. She has been a public relations director, journalist and feature writer, developing a talent for creative writing which she has shared with ACTING UP! As a person who loves to take on new challenges, she is never afraid to take a risk and go "out on a limb." Not even a broken hip could hold her down.

One time in an improvisation I played a Southern girl. It was great. It felt glorious! I was very happy because for once, I proved that I could act. Everyone liked it. The group was wonderful, so enthusiastic about my accomplishment. It was like riding the crest of a wave.

Joe Sonntag

Joe's retirement from his former work as a chiropractor has motivated him to be busier than ever. When he is not traveling extensively throughout the United States lecturing for the Amateur Organist Association International, he is busy creating new programs for older adults. His previous show business career as a ventriloquist and magician has made him a "natural" for ACTING UP!

There are some inhibitions you can't get rid of. There is a lot of therapy in ACTING UP! There are more women than men, but I like it that way. As with anyone's future, no one knows what the future holds. We play it by ear day-to-day, from month to month. Whatever comes up we improvise. We never know what's going to come of it.

Bernice Weiss

Bernice speaks quietly but "carries a big stick." She has a degree in education and has worked as a teacher, as a librarian, and for her husband. Her original observations and clever turns of mind continually add stimulus to ACTING UP!'s material. A wife and mother most of her adult life, Bernice is finding that theatre is where she always belonged. She has found her sense of humor and her anger on stage, and she loves it.

I was recruited through ACTING UP! for a session at a university for a group of students specifically interested in the psychology of aging. I remember saying that we can still make big changes in our lives when we're in our sixties. Many students remarked afterwards that they got more out of that one session than they had the entire course. What was most important to me was that they no longer were afraid of getting old. In ACTING UP! we are given the feeling we are wanted, we aren't being judged and there is no competition to be the best.

Shirley Helfand (1919-1982)

Shirley was a widow for many years. She was a "trouper" in every sense of the word. Her bright spirit remains part of ACTING UP! Shirley's daughter, Faith Helfand Karm, shared these thoughts with us:

Everyone in the family knew that Mondays were ACTING UP! days. My mother had said this a million times, "Put on your Pagliacci Face and go on the stage." Her life was hard, but she spent most of it going along with a smile. Believe me, she had to be a good actress to do that because illness and difficulty made it hard to smile. She enjoyed the love and recognition, a vein that so often runs through all actors. When we were in stores together, people would come out of the blue and say to her, "I saw you in ACTING UP!" She accepted this, not boastfully, but with a quiet inward recognition.

BIBLIOGRAPHY

BOOKS

Achenbaum, Andrew. *Images of Old Age in America, 1970 to the Present*. Ann Arbor: University of Michigan - Wayne State University Press, 1978.

Berlin, Anne and Paul. *Learning Through Movement*. Los Angeles: Ward-Ritchie Press, 1971.

Burger, Isabel. *Creative Drama for Senior Adults*. Wilton, Connecticut: Morehouse-Barlow, 1980.

Burnside, Irene M. *Working with the Elderly, Group Processes and Techniques*. North Scituate, Massachusetts: Duxbury Press, 1977.

Butler, Robert N. *Why Survive Being Old In America?* New York: Harper and Row, 1975.

Caine, Lynn. *Widow*. New York: William Morrow and Company, 1974.

Cohen, Robert. *Acting Power*. Palo Alto, California: Mayfield Publishing Co., 1978.

Comfort, Alex. *A Good Age*. New York: Crown Publishers, Inc., 1976.

Cornish, Roger and Kase, C. Robert., Eds. *Senior Adult Theatre*. University Park: The Penn State University Press, 1981.

De Beauvoir, Simone, *Coming of Age*. translated by Patrick O'Brian. New York: Putnam, 1972.

Downs, Hugh. *Thirty Dirty Lies About Old*. Niles, Illinois: Argus Communications, 1979.

Epstein and Mendelsohn, R. *Record and Remember: Tracing Your Roots Through Oral History*. New York: Simon & Schuster, 1978.

Fischer, David. *Growing Old In America*. New York: Oxford University Press, 1978.

Gray, Paula. *Dramatics for the Elderly*. New York: Columbia Teachers College Press, 1974.

Glasser, William. *The Identity Society*. New York: Harper and Row, 1972.

181

Harner, Michael. *The Way of the Shaman*. San Francisco: Harper & Row, 1980.

Hawley, Robert. *Value Exploration Through Role Playing*. New York: Hart Publishing Co, 1975.

Hayes, Helen with Dody, Sanford. *On Reflection*. (Autobiography) New York: M. Evans, distributed by Lippincott, 1968.

Hodge, Francis. *Play Directing Analysis and Communication*. Englewood Cliffs, New Jersey: Prentice Hall, 1971.

Hodgson, John Reed and Richards, Ernest. *Improvisation: Discovery and Creativity in Drama*. London: Methuen, 1966.

Huyck, Margaret. *Growing Older*. Englewood Cliffs, New Jersey: Prentice Hall, 1974.

Kaminsky, Marc. *What's Inside You It Shines Out of You*. New York: Horizon, 1974.

Kelly, Elizabeth Y. *The Magic If*. Baltimore, Maryland: National Educational Press, 1972.

Koch, Kenneth. *I Never Told Anybody...: Teaching People Poetry Writing in a Nursing Home*. New York: Random House, 1977.

Larrain, Virginai, ed. *Timeless Voices, A Poetry Anthology Celebration, the Fulfillment of Age*. Melbra, California: Celestial Arts, 1978.

Le Shan, Eda. *The Wonderful Crisis of Middle Age*. New York: Warner Paperback Library, 1973.

Luce, Gay G. *Your Second Life: Vitality in Middle and Later Age*. New York: Delacorte, 1979.

McCaslin, Nellie. *Creative Dramatics in the Classroom*. New York: David McKay Co., 1974.

Michaels, Claire. "Geridrama, Drama Therapy with Senior Citizens," in Vol. II, *Drama in Therapy*. ed. by Gertrude Schaffner and Richard Courtney. New York: Drama Book Specialists, 1979.

Miller, S. *Psychology of Play*. Baltimore, Maryland: Penguin Books, 1968.

Montagu, Ashley. *Touching: The Human Significance of the Skin*. New York: Columbia University Press, 1971.

Perlstein, Susan. *A Stage for Memory*. New York: Teachers and Writers Collaborative, 1982.

Peterson, James and Briley, Michael L. *Widows and Widowhood*. Chicago: Follett Publishing Company, 1977.

Satir, Virginia. *People Making*. Palo Alto, California: Science and Behavior Books, Inc., 1972.

Sawyer, Ruth. *The Way of the Storyteller*. New York: Viking Press, 1942.

Schattner, G. and Courtney, Richard, Eds. *Drama in Therapy*. New York: Drama Book Specialists, 1979. (See Claire Michaels chapter,

182

"Geridrama for Senior Citizens.")
Schuckman, Terry. *Aging Is Not For Sissies*. Philadelphia: Westminster Press, 1975.
Shurtleff, Michael. *Audition*. New York: Bantam Press, 1980.
Silverstein, Lee M. *Consider the Alternative*. Minneapolis, Minnesota: Comp Care Publications, 1980.
Spolin, Viola. *Improvisations for the Theatre*. Chicago: Northwestern University Press, 1963.
Sunderland, Jacqueline, ed. *Arts and the Aging: An Agenda for Action*. Washington, D.C.: National Council on Aging, 1977.
Way, Brian. *Development Through Drama*. New York: Humanities Press, 1967.
Zarit, Steven, ed. *Readings in Aging and Death, Contemporary Perspectives*. New York: Harper & Row, 1977.

PLAYS AND STORIES FOR PERFORMANCE

Albee, Edward. *The Sandbox* and *The American Dream*. New York: Coward, McCann & Geoghegan, Inc., 1960.
Ancona, George. *Growing Older*. New York: E. P. Dutton, 1978.
Anderson, Robert. "I'm Herbert." in *I Can't Hear You When the Water is Running*. New York: Random House, 1967.
Balzac, Honoré de. *Old Man Goriot*. ed. by Somerset Maugham. Philadelphia: Winston, 1949.
Beckett, Samuel. *Endgame*. New York: Grove Press, Inc., 1958.
Bermant, Chaim. *Diary of An Old Man*. New York: Holt, Rinehart and Winston, 1967.
Cather, Willa. *Death Comes for the Archbishop*. New York: Knopf, 1966.
Cervantes-Saavedra, Miguel d. *Don Quixote*. New York: Viking Press, 1949.
Chekhov, Anton Pavlovich. *The Cherry Orchard, The Seagull, Uncle Vanya*, in *Plays*. Baltimore: Penguin Books, 1959.
Coburn, D. L. *The Gin Game*. New York: Drama Book Specialists, 1978.
Cornish, Roger and Orlock, John. *Short Plays for the Long Living*. Boston: Baker's Plays, 1976.
Cristofer, Michael. *The Shadow Box*. New York: Drama Book Specialists, 1977.
Denker, Henry. *Second Time Around*. New York: Samuel French, Inc., 1977.

Diggs, Elizabeth. *Close Ties*. Garden City, New York: Nelson Doubleday, Inc., 1981.

Farber, Norma. *How Does It Feel to Be Old?* New York: E. P. Dutton, 1979.

Figes, Eva. *Winter Journey*. New York: Hill & Wang, 1967.

Giraudoux, Jean. *The Madwoman of Chaillot* in Vol. I, *Four Plays*. New York: Hill & Wang, Inc., 1972.

James, Henry. *The Aspern Papers*. New York: New Directions, 1950.

_____

"The Jolly Corner," in *The Novels and Tales*. New York: Scribner, 1961-64.

Kaminsky, Marc. *The Book of Autobiographies*. New York: Teachers and Writers Collaborative, Inc., 1982.

Kawabata, Wasuari. *House of Sleeping Beauties*. Rutland, Vermont: Tuttle, 1969.

_____

Sound of the Mountain. Rutland, Vermont: Tuttle, 1970.

Leonard, Hugh. *Da*. New York: Samuel French, Inc., 1973.

Long, Arthur Sumner. *Never Too Late*. New York: Samuel French, Inc., 1963.

Mann, Thomas. *Black Swan*. New York: Knopf, Inc., 1954.

Mannes, Marya. *They*. Garden City, New York: Doubleday, 1968.

Masters, Edgar Lee. *Spoon River Anthology*. New York: Macmillan Publishing Co., Inc., 1968.

McNeil, Janet. *The Small Widow*. New York: Athenaeum Publishers, 1968.

Olive, John. *Clara's Play*. (unpublished) New York: Susan Schulman, Agent, 1982.

Olson, Tillie. *Tell Me a Riddle*. New York: Dell Publishing Co., 1976.

Osborn, Paul. *Mornings at Seven*. New York: Samuel French, Inc., 1940.

Shakespeare, William. *King Lear*. ed. by T. J. Spencer. New York: Penguin, 1981.

Simon, Neil. *Sunshine Boys*. New York: Samuel French, Inc., 1973.

Spark, Muriel. *Momento Mori*. Cleveland: The World Publishing Co., 1958.

Thompson, Ernest. *On Golden Pond*. New York: Dodd, Mead & Co., 1979.

Tolstoy, Leo. *The Death of Ivan Ilych*. New York: Bantam Books, Inc., 1981.

Updike, John. *The Poorhouse Fair*. Greenwich, Connecticut: Fawcett Publications, 1981.

Woolf, Douglas. *Fade Out*. New York: Grove Press, 1959.

POST SCRIPT

ACTING UP! is a special improvisational theatre group made up of people all over age sixty-five who write and perform original materials. The thirteen members present a humorous, sometimes outspoken and always energetic poke at the stereotypes and myths of ageism. At the same time they share their philosophy that growing older can be a time of self-discovery and creativity.

The company, as one of the pioneering troupes of older adult performers, has been fortunate to receive notice in several television tapings. CBS's Chicago newsmagazine, *Two on Two,* taped an intergenerational program which caught the reactions of high school students to the older performers. WGN-TV broadcast the Company's fifteen-minute Christmas play, *A Christmas Carol for Seniors.* NBC's local affiliate station has hosted members of the ACTING UP! company in local and affiliate programming. In April, 1982, the entire company performed for the National Council on Aging's Annual Conference in Washington, D.C.

ACTING UP! offers workshops which demonstrate the creative drama skills and techniques the group uses in its work with (and as) older adults. In the six years that ACTING UP! has been together, its members have developed some specially-tailored processes for stimulating creativity from elders, and from people with disabling conditions. During a two-hour workshop, topics covered include:

Why drama for elders?

Getting organized

Leadership skills

Storytelling and oral history

Improvisations and theatre games

Intergenerational aspects

Problem-solving skills

185

The company is available for booking. For information, or to arrange an engagement, contact:

Special Community Programs Assistant
Oakton Community College
1600 Ed. Golf Road
Des Plaines, IL 60016
(312) 635-1977

The authors are available for workshops and in-service training. For information contact:

Marcie Telander
2005 N. Mohawk
Chicago, Illinois 60614
(312) 528-5466

Two documentary films explore the growth and development of the ACTING UP! company:

ACTING UP! (30 minutes - 1977) A documentary of an improvisational drama company made up of non-professional actors, all over sixty-five, reveals the powerful therapeutic tools of supportive group discussion, creative expression and dramatic role-playing. Produced and directed by Marcie Telander and Mark Schwiesow. Available from FilmComm, 108 W. Grand Avenue, Chicago, IL 60610.

These are the Days (20 minutes - 1982) The film explores the rich lives of two members of the ACTING UP! company, using the theatrical group as a background. It portrays the positive and enriching aspects of growing older. Produced and directed by Emmy Award winners, Kier Cline and Barry Teicher. Available from Film Ideas, Inc., 1155 Laurel Avenue, Deerfield, IL 60015.

It has become apparent from our experience that newspaper and television feature writers and producers are interested in covering older adults to discover how they spend their time. Since the players are aware and vocal on the subject of a rich and rewarding life after retirement, the media is interested in exploring the options.

What do people do with their lives beyond work and family? What can we look forward to when we retire? ACTING UP!